Things Atheists Say

that simply make no sense.

Patrick Prill

FIDELIS
PUBLISHING

FIDELIS PUBLISHING
ISBN: 978-1-7354285-0-5
ISBN (eBook): 978-1-7354285-3-6

Things Atheists Say
That simply make no sense
© 2021 Patrick Prill

Cover Design by Patrick Prill

This publisher is not responsible for the departures chosen by this author from trade book publishing standards as set by The Chicago Manual of Style.

Fidelis Publishing, LLC Sterling, VA • Nashville, TN fidelispublishing.com

Published in the United States of America

For my incredible children and their generation, with special thanks to Michael as my motivation and many thanks to Jennifer, Rebecca, Jim, Dan, Nate, Willow, Ed, Justin, Rick, Bryan and Michael for their many helpful comments and suggestions.

CONTENTS

INTRODUCTION

A theists are only human. That can be said of us all. None of us are perfect and we don't always "get it right." And, even when we are right about something, we may not always express it in the most gracious manner. After all, we're only human.

This book isn't about atheists. It's about some of the things they say. When you listen to what many well-known atheists are saying, it can be surprising. It's surprising because much of what they say actually makes no sense. In some cases, this is because it's simply not true. In others, it's based on wishful thinking, filled with logical fallacies, biased, or just very uninformed. However, something said even with intellectual or emotional resolve doesn't necessarily make it so.

This book is also not really about science, though science is included in the topics covered. It seems that theists, atheists and agnostics can all be great scientists. Yet even great scientists can get a few things wrong and it's certain they don't always agree. That's also true of great historians, philosophers, ethics professors and theologians.

No one is infallible. We can all make mistakes in logic, draw from sources that got the facts wrong and be blinded to truth by our own limited perspectives. So, we shouldn't belittle each other when we get it wrong. But, we should be able and willing to kindly challenge each other's facts, reasoning and conclusions. That's what this book seeks to do.

About 3.1 percent of Americans are atheists. Another 4 percent are agnostic and aren't sure if God exists or not.[1] That leaves about 93 percent of Americans who believe there is a God or a higher power. This book is for all of you.

As for those who are quoted in this book—should I ever meet them—I hope that, though disagreeing, I may not have been found to have misrepresented them or been unkind to them. It seems that in today's society we can either engage in civil discourse or civil war. I choose the former.

---

[1] *Religious Landscape Study* (Washington, DC: Pew Research Center, 2014), http://www.pewforum.org/religious-landscape-study/.

THE UNIVERSE
AND LIFE

THE UNIVERSE LOOKS DESIGNED, BUT IT'S NOT

But the discovery relatively recently of the extreme fine-tuning of so many of the laws of nature could lead at least some of us back to the old idea that this grand design is the work of some grand designer. . . .That is not the answer of modern science.[2]

Because there is a law like gravity, the universe can and will create itself from nothing. . . . Spontaneous creation is the reason there is something rather than nothing, why the universe exists, why we exist. It is not necessary to invoke God to light the blue touch paper and set the universe going.[3]

—Stephen Hawking

The late Stephen Hawking was a brilliant man. He was a physicist and cosmologist with a PhD from Cambridge. Most people know about him from his best-selling

---

[2]Stephen Hawking, *The Grand Design* (New York: Bantam Books, 2012), 164.
[3]Ibid., 180.

3

books, *A Brief History of Time and The Grand Design* and the movie about his life, *The Theory of Everything*. Stephen Hawking was very intelligent, but some of his ideas contradicted his intellect and exposed a huge bias.

Hawking observed that the laws of nature and the many incredibly fine-tuned variables, making life on earth possible, look as though they were designed. However, he dismissed even the possibility of a designer as being **unscientific**. Instead, he devised a theory not requiring a designer.

Hawking theorized that the universe spontaneously came into being from nothing *"because there is a law like gravity."* In other words, the universe had to create itself from nothing because of the law of gravity. He then added, since the probability that a life-supporting universe like ours exists is so incredibly small, there must be an almost infinite number of spontaneously self-generated universes for even one like ours to exist.

This is some theory. There are a few obvious problems with it. The first is, it isn't actually based on science. George Ellis, another brilliant physicist, who co-authored *The Large Scale Structure of Space-Time* with Stephen Hawking, states that Hawking's multiverse idea is **unprovable** and **philosophical**. He further states that, even if there were many universes, preexisting laws would be required to make them come into existence. There would have to be **something** that required universes to come into being.[4] So, it seems Stephen Hawking's scientific theory for how the universe came to be isn't really scientific after all—it's philosophical.

---

[4]John Horgan, "Physicist George Ellis Knocks Physicists for Knocking Philosophy, Falsification, Free Will," *Scientific American* (July 22, 2014), https://blogs.scientificamerican.com/cross-check/physicist-george-ellis-knocks-physicists-for-knocking-philosophy-falsification-free-will/.

Paul Davies, a professor of mathematical physics, observes that *"the entire scientific enterprise is predicated on the assumption that there are reasons for why things are as they are."*[5] He likens the multiverse idea's lack of substance in providing a reason for the universe's existence to be like a mythical super-turtle holding up the world:

> So the multiverse likewise retains an element of arbitrariness and absurdity. Its super-turtle also levitates for no reasons, so that theory too is ultimately absurd.[6]

John Lennox, a mathematics professor at Oxford,[7] also points out several simple logical fallacies in Stephen Hawking's reasoning. The first is, **nothing cannot spontaneously create anything.** If there is nothing, then there is no cause, material, laws of nature, necessity or reason—there is **nothing.** Stating that nothing will do something (create itself) from nothing (itself) by necessity because of the existence of something (gravity) is a logically absurd statement.[8]

Lennox concludes, *"What all this goes to show is that nonsense is still nonsense, even when talked by world-famous scientists."*[9] Lennox also states that, even if there were many universes, it still wouldn't negate the possibility that God was their cause.[10]

---

[5]Paul Davies, *The Goldilocks Enigma* (Boston: Houghton Mifflin Co., 2006), 218.
[6]Ibid.
[7]John Lennox is a Professor of Mathematics (emeritus) at Oxford University. He earned a DPhil from Oxford, a PhD from Cambridge and a DSc from Cardiff.
[8]John Lennox, *God and Stephen Hawking* (Oxford, England: Lion Hudson, 2011), 29–32.
[9]Ibid., 32.
[10]Ibid., 47–50.

Stephen Hawking was correct—the universe does look designed. It looks so designed that Freeman Dyson, a Princeton University physicist, famously observed:

> *The more I examine the universe and study the details of its architecture, the more evidence I find that the universe in some sense knew we were coming.*[11]

Science points to a beginning of our universe. There was nothing—no time, matter, energy, space or laws—then there was everything. We call this the "big bang." And, the everything that resulted is subject to precisely tuned laws enabling (and possibly compelling) life to exist.

Science can't prove what caused all this. However, it seems logical that the natural universe couldn't have created itself from nothing any more than we could have given birth to ourselves (before we existed) from nothing.

Hawking was inconsistent in his logic. He dismissed the possibility that our fine-tuned universe may have a designer, who exists outside of nature, as unscientific. Yet his own theory isn't based on science—it's a philosophical speculation. And, his idea of universes creating themselves out of nothing is fraught with logical problems. Even to many other physicists and mathematicians, this makes no sense.

---

[11]Freeman Dyson, *Disturbing the Universe* (New York: Basic Books, 1979), 250.

LIFE LOOKS DESIGNED, BUT IT'S NOT

The observed fact is that every species, and every organ that has ever been looked at within every species, is good at what it does.[12]
We live on a planet where we are surrounded by perhaps ten million species, each one of which independently displays a powerful illusion of apparent design.[13]

—Richard Dawkins

It's amazing. Every species and every organ within every species on planet Earth look designed. There are no life forms or organs within life forms that don't do what they do well. That's ten million species that look like they were designed and none that don't. Yet Richard Dawkins, an Oxford professor and world-renowned biologist, contends that this ten million-to-zero ratio happened without any

---

[12]Richard Dawkins, *The God Delusion* (New York: Mariner Books, 2008), 167.
[13]Ibid.

guidance from a designer. He says it just *looks* like it was designed—it's an illusion.

What would cause us to conclude something had been designed? Six of the most common indicators would likely be whether the thing in question possessed beauty, symmetry and precision, complexity, information, logic and purpose. If something possessed all of these attributes, such as a modern skyscraper, it would be reasonable to conclude it was designed. However, a rock formation, which may be beautiful, symmetrical and somewhat complex, would be less likely to have been designed—especially if an alternate cause, such as wind erosion, is evident.

Using this as a starting point, humans and animals do look as though they were designed—they possess beauty, symmetry and precision, complexity, information, logic and purpose. However, to avoid simple conclusions, let's look deeper and use a few other examples of design as a frame of reference.

Computer programs—How complex does a computer program need to be for us to determine its origin was a programmer? How large a database? How complex the database schema? How many functions? How many stored procedures? How many lines of code? How elegant and efficient the logic? How much integration with other programs? How elaborate the build instructions? You probably get the point—right?

This frame of reference was one of the factors that caused Antony Flew, one of the world's leading atheist philosophers to change his mind. He observed that DNA, the building block of life, operates like a program. Each strand of human DNA contains a database of about 3.1 billion characters of **coded information** that also operates as a **language** and contains **logical programs** that are **purposeful** and **self-replicating**. He concluded that its cause was beyond biology—there had to be a designer:

> *The philosophical question that has not been answered in origin-of-life studies is this: How can a universe of mindless matter produce beings with intrinsic ends, self-replication capabilities and "coded chemistry." Here we are not dealing with biology, but an entirely different category of problem.*[14]

Is Antony Flew correct? After all, he was a philosopher not a scientist—right? Let's look at another analogy.

Production lines – An automobile production line is pretty amazing. Raw materials are shipped in from all over the world, parts are fabricated and then sent to plants where they're assembled and tested. People use complex machines, robots and their own brute force in a precise production process that results in beautiful new cars rolling off the assembly line. This is also sort of how each human cell operates.

Bruce Alberts, the former head of the National Academy of Sciences, observed:

> *. . . we now know that nearly every major process in a cell is carried out by assemblies of 10 or more protein molecules. And, as it carries out its biological functions, each of these protein assemblies interacts with several other large complexes of*

---

[14]Antony Flew, *There Is a God* (New York: HarperCollins, 2007), 124.

proteins. Indeed, the entire cell can be viewed as a factory that contains an elaborate network of interlocking assembly lines, each of which is composed of a set of large protein machines.[15]

Michael Behe, a biology professor at Lehigh University, points out that the machines in each human cell must assemble themselves—sort of like pouring out automobile parts on the floor only to see them become a car all by themselves. Cells make their own parts and internal machines. They use twenty kinds of amino acids to make proteins that then bind to other proteins to make the machines in the cell. These machines operate with each other to perform various functions and make new cells.

For two proteins to bind to each other, they have to have complimentary shapes and chemical properties.[16] However, most cellular machines are composed of many proteins—that's a lot of precise connections.

Michael Behe places the probability of protein complexes with just two binding sites successfully occurring randomly at 1 in 10^{40}. He states that 10^{40} (ten with forty zeroes behind it) is likely more than all the cells that have ever existed in the world in the last four billion years and concludes:

The immediate, most important implication is that complexes with more than two binding sites—ones that require three or more different kinds of proteins—are beyond the edge of evolution, past what is biologically reasonable to expect Darwinian evolution to have accomplished. . . . the odds are against a single event of

---

[15]Michael Behe, *The Edge of Evolution* (New York: Free Press, 2008), 125.
[16]Ibid., 123–35.

*this variety in the history of life. It is biologically
unreasonable.*[17]

The improbability of cellular machines randomly constructing themselves from proteins is just one of the factors causing Mr. Behe to conclude that cell structures didn't evolve unaided. To him, the logical conclusion is that they were aided by a designer.

In looking at just the two examples of a computer program and an auto assembly line, it's easy to see why we conclude they were designed. It's also easy to see the parallels between programs and assembly lines and the processes that exist in each human cell.

WHAT ABOUT ALTERNATE CAUSES?

Are there any possible ways life could have emerged and constructed itself without the aid of a designer? Have scientists found a possible natural cause? It seems that the current answer is no. Stephen Meyer, a Cambridge University educated PhD, observes that theories seeking to explain how life forms could have constructed themselves have all failed:

> . . . *self-organizational theories have failed to identify known physical and chemical processes capable of generating the information present in actual living systems.*[18]

Yet, even though there are no workable theories to explain how life could have emerged unaided and how complex

---

[17]Ibid., 146.
[18]Stephen Meyer, *Darwin's Doubt* (New York: HarperOne, 2013), 310.

living things could have constructed themselves, Richard Dawkins is adamant that life on Earth was not designed.

This is in spite of his own observation that all of the ten million species on Earth appear to be designed and none do not. He takes this position because he believes another alternative—a purely natural explanation—could have been the cause. He attributes it to **natural selection.**

Mr. Dawkins calls natural selection *"a generalized process for optimizing biological species."*[19] He seems to use the term broadly to describe genetic variation, natural selection and genetic inheritance. And, scientists have, in fact, observed a variety of types of genetic variation.

Yet does it make sense to attribute the origination of life to a process which he states merely optimizes species? After all, no theories for how life could have emerged and organized itself have presently worked. And does it really make sense to dismiss the possibility that life had a designer, when the probability for even simple protein machines in cells existing by chance is beyond the probabilities biology can offer?

It seems it does not.

---

[19] Dawkins, *The God Delusion*, 167.

NATURAL SELECTION ANSWERS EVERYTHING!

Natural selection not only explains the whole of life; it also raises our consciousness to the power of science to explain how organized complexity can emerge from simple beginnings without any deliberate guidance.[20]

—Richard Dawkins

To Richard Dawkins, the existence of a biological process called natural selection answers all of life's riddles. It answers how life emerged. It explains the existence of so many species of animals. It explains morality. It even explains why you exist. It explains everything!

Well, it almost explains everything. Mr. Dawkins also states that natural selection needed some kind of genetic material and some luck to get it started. He also concedes that it needed more luck to jump over huge improbable chasms to make the origin of life, the formation of cells and

---

[20]Richard Dawkins, *The God Delusion* (New York: Mariner Books, 2008), 141.

consciousness possible.[21] So, it seems that natural selection doesn't really answer **everything**. It seems some kind of genetic material and multiple rounds of luck are needed too.

Most scientists readily point out that natural selection, as described by Charles Darwin, does not fully explain the origins of life or the observed evolution of species. And, Neo-Darwinism—which includes variation, natural selection and the ability to inherit variations with the knowledge of genes—doesn't explain the origins of life or fully answer the evolution of species either.

So where do natural selection and Neo-Darwinism fall short; what do they not answer?

The list is actually fairly long but let's take a quick look at eight ways Neo-Darwinism falls short of answers:

1. *Prior information*—Fred Hoyle, a brilliant and sometimes controversial astronomer and former agnostic, rejected natural selection as a means of answering how life emerged and developed on Earth because information is needed to precede it.

   No matter how large the environment one considers, life cannot have had a random beginning. . . . Just as the brain of Shakespeare was necessary to produce famous plays, so prior information was necessary to produce a living cell.[22]

   In the last chapter, we saw that the probability of a simple protein machine inside a cell being constructed by chance is beyond what is biologically reasonable.

   How probable is it that an entire simple cell could be assembled by chance? Stephen Meyer places the

---

[21]Ibid., 168–69.
[22]Sir Fred Hoyle and Chandra Wickramasinghe, *Evolution from Space* (New York: Touchstone, 1981), 148.

probability at 1 in 10^{40861}—a number massively greater than all of the protons, electrons, and neutrons in all the atoms in the entire known universe, which is estimated at 10^{80}.[23] He concludes:

In other words, the universe itself does not possess the probabilistic resources necessary to render probable the origin of biological information by chance alone.[24]

Evolutionary processes can't explain how the information that's required for life to exist originated. However, the chance of it occurring randomly is essentially zero.

2. **Origins**—Francis Crick, one of the discoverers of the DNA double helix, has famously stated:

    An honest man, armed with all the knowledge available to us now, could only state that in some sense, the origin of life appears at the moment to be almost a miracle, so many are the conditions which would have had to have been satisfied to get it going.[25]

    That was in 1981. Yet scientists today still can't provide an answer. Natural selection, by definition, can't answer the question of the origin of life. That's because natural selection can only occur if life already exists.

3. **Self-replication**—It is not enough for information, DNA or even life to exist; the very first living cell had to possess the capability to replicate itself. Richard Dawkins doesn't know how this happened, but assumes it was "somehow, as a consequence of the

---

[23]Stephen Meyer, *Signature in the Cell* (New York: HarperOne, 2009), 212, 219.
[24]Ibid., 219.
[25]Francis Crick, *Life Itself: Its Origin and Nature* (New York: Simon & Schuster, 1981), 88.

ordinary laws of physics."[26] Again, natural selection can't provide the answer because self-replication had to precede it.

4. *Rapid development of life*—Scientists convey that, about 500 million years ago, there was a rapid appearance of a massive number of complex life-forms on earth. If natural selection relies on a slow process of genetic variation, how did they appear so rapidly? Scientists are working on the question, but they don't currently know the answer. One theory is that genes are biologically preprogrammed with the ability to adapt rapidly under certain conditions. However, that leaves the question, how did these programs originate? Again, natural selection and Neo-Darwinism can't provide an answer.[27]

5. *Purpose*—Jacques Monod, a biochemist and Nobel Prize winner, states that biological structures and processes demonstrate purpose. However, biology can't answer why.[28]

6. *Consciousness*—Sam Harris, a very vocal atheist with a PhD in neuroscience, has concluded that science will likely never answer how consciousness came into existence.[29]

7. *Human Intellect*—Susumu Ohno, an evolutionary biologist, stated that even ancient cave-dwelling humans possessed the genes necessary to compose complex music and write profound novels. However, their environments didn't require them to do so.[30] How then did this occur?

---

[26]Richard Dawkins, *The Blind Watchmaker* (New York: W.W. Horton, 1996), 183.

[27]Stephen Meyer, *Darwin's Doubt* (New York: HarperOne, 2013), 292–335.

[28]Jacques Monod, *Chance and Necessity* (New York: Alfred A. Knopf, 1971), 13–21.

[29]Sam Harris, *The End of Faith* (New York: W.W. Horton & Co., 2005), 208.

[30]Sir Fred Hoyle, *The Intelligent Universe* (New York: Holt, Reinhart and Winston, 1983), 229.

8. *Mental algorithms*—The human brain is an organic computer. It receives, stores, recalls and processes information and then reaches conclusions, which it also stores. Yet Roger Penrose, one of the world's most highly regarded mathematical physicists, has concluded that the mental programs (algorithms) the mind employs could not just be the product of natural selection:

> ... *I am a strong believer in the power of natural selection. But I do not see how natural selection, in itself, can evolve algorithms which could have the kind of conscious judgements of the validity of other algorithms that we seem to have.*[31]

In looking at just these eight examples, Dawkins' statement that natural selection answers everything falls far short of being compelling. In fact, even other atheists don't agree with him. Thomas Nagel, a philosophy professor, states:

> *One of the tendencies it* [the cosmic authority problem] *supports is the ludicrous overuse of evolutionary biology to explain everything about life; including everything about the human mind.*[32]

It seems that Richard Dawkins is overzealous in his claim that natural selection is the answer to all the mysteries of existence and life. Evolutionary processes are real. However, natural selection certainly doesn't answer everything.[33]

---

[31]Roger Penrose, *The Emperor's New Mind* (Oxford, England: Oxford University Press, 2016), 535.

[32]Thomas Nagel, *The Last Word* (New York: Oxford University Press, 1997), 131.

[33]Richard Dawkins admits that there is one more thing natural selection can't answer—itself: "*We still don't know exactly how natural selection began on earth.*" *The Blind Watch Maker*, 237.

OUR UNIVERSE MIGHT JUST BE A COMPUTER SIMULATION

*Moderator Neil deGrasse Tyson, director
of the museum's Hayden Planetarium, put
the odds at 50-50 that our entire existence
is a program on someone else's hard drive.
"I think the likelihood may be very high,"
he said. . . . Somewhere out there could be a
being whose intelligence is that much greater
than our own. "We would be drooling, blith-
ering idiots in their presence," he said. "If
that's the case, it is easy for me to imagine
that everything in our lives is just a creation of
some other entity for their entertainment."[34]*

Neil deGrasse Tyson is a popular astrophysicist. He has written books, does live shows on stage, appears on television and is the director of the planetarium at the American Museum of Natural History. He also has a PhD

---

[34]Clara Moskowitz, "Are We Living in a Computer Simulation?", *Scientific American*, April 7, 2016, https://www.scientificamerican.com/article/are-we-living-in-a-computer-simulation/.

from Columbia University and seems to be very smart. Yet, while he sees the odds that our universe is a more intelligent being's computer simulation as fifty-fifty, he seems to place the odds that God exists at zero. Why is that?

Why is it that even intelligent scientists can more easily conceive of a cause for our existence and that of the universe as being something from science fiction rather than even acknowledge the **possibility** that the cause could be God?

Scientific materialism is the idea that everything has a physical cause and nothing nonphysical exists. It's a philosophical point of view.[35] It's philosophical because it can't really be proven. After all, in a physical world, it's tough to set up a scientific test that goes beyond what is physical.

As a philosophical view, materialism results in the tendency to accept any possible physical cause of the universe as plausible and any nonphysical cause as implausible.

Neil deGrasse Tyson seems to be a good example of a scientist who sees the world through the eyes of scientific materialism. To conclude that our existence could actually be playing out on someone's computer hard drive is a novel idea. It would imply a highly intelligent **material** being beyond our realm of existence who programmed it and sustains its operation.

This hardly seems to be more probable than the existence of God. Yet Tyson gives the possibility of God's existence no merit. Let's all just hope the hard drive doesn't crash.

DOES THE NONPHYSICAL EXIST?

Colin McGinn puts into question whether the physical is all there is. He's a British philosopher who holds to atheism

---

[35]Scientific materialism is also called physicalism.

and who now lives in America. In a recent essay, he conveyed that physics isn't necessarily just about the physical.

The physical thus exists against a background of completely non-physical things. If anything, space and time belong on the side of God, not on the side of matter (consider their infinity and eternality)—at least as Newton sees things. . . . The relationship between physics and the physical is actually quite contentious; certainly, we must not assume that what physics deals with is ipso facto *physical in any well-defined sense.*[36]

What would you call things that exist but aren't physical? Theists might call them spiritual, but they could just as easily be called the "nonphysical but real." And, if there is a set of things that are nonphysical but real, could God not be in that category and also be their source?

Rupert Sheldrake, a Cambridge educated biochemist, takes it one step further. He not only challenges the materialism of the early 1900s and the many who still hold to it, he calls it *"a belief system that governs conventional scientific thinking"* and calls it *"an act of faith, grounded in nineteenth-century ideology."*[37] He contends that this view of the world is now holding science back.

Scientists have generally been of the mind-set that we should make conclusions based upon where the evidence leads us. However, to explore the existence of our universe and the existence of life and limit the search to the box of

[36]Colin McGinn, "Physics and Physicalism," January 28, 2019, http://www.colin mcginn.net/physics-and-physicalism/#.XNWKYRRKhpg.
[37]Rupert Sheldrake, *The Science Delusion: Freeing the Spirit of Enquiry* (London, England: Hodder & Stoughton, 2012), 7.

scientific materialism, seems to exclude a huge realm of possibilities. Does it really make sense to do that?

WHAT ABOUT PARTICLE PHYSICS?

Particle physics is the level of material things that are smaller than atoms.[38] It's the peculiar layer of material things where virtual particles seem to come into existence and then disappear (violating the law of conservation of energy).[39]

Scientists are trying to comprehend how particle physics works, but the other rules of physics don't seem to apply. It's a different layer that's sort of one between material existence and nonexistence. And, if this is the layer between material existence and nonexistence, is there a layer deeper than that?

IS THE UNIVERSE REALLY CLOSED?

The fundamental challenge with materialism is, material things don't necessarily come from material things. Our universe actually consists of tiny particles that appear and disappear. It had a beginning (the big bang) and its source was evidently nonmaterial. Even stranger, the universe is continually expanding—into nothing.

---

[38]Particle physics' subatomic realm includes: protons, neurons, electrons and the smaller particles that comprise them. Protons and neutrons are comprised of six "flavors" of quarks with corresponding anti-quarks and gluons, which hold the quarks together. Electrons and quarks are fundamental particles and so are photons, of which light is comprised. And there's much more. It's note-worthy that classical mechanics doesn't seem to explain the actions and interactions of these particles.

[39]Gordon Kane, "Are virtual particles really constantly popping in and out of existence? Or are they merely a mathematical bookkeeping device for quantum mechanics?", *Scientific American*, October 9, 2006, https://www.scientificamerican.com/article/are-virtual-particles-rea/?redirect=1.

And, as we'll discuss later, the amount of dark energy in the universe (the energy field filling empty space) is actually increasing![40] How is this possible, if the universe is a finite set of material things?

Many scientists in the early 1900s thought the notion of matter and energy having a beginning was ludicrous.[41] After all, the "law" of preservation of matter and energy suggested this is impossible. But it happened—and matter and energy, space, time and laws of physics also had a beginning. Their source was nonmaterial as well. So just maybe there are nonmaterial things that are real.

Gerald Schroeder, an MIT educated physicist, sums it up this way:

> *The physical system we refer to as our universe is not closed to the nonphysical. It cannot be closed. Its total beginning required a nonphysical act. Call it the big bang. Call it creation. Let the creating force be a potential field if the idea of God is bothersome to you, but realize the fact that the nonphysical gave rise to the physical.[42]*

Is the nonphysical realm the realm of God? This possibility seems to be more in keeping with what we actually know about the universe than computer simulations.

That might make more sense.

---

[40] Scientists now believe that the expansion of the universe and the constancy of dark energy, which counteracts gravity, suggests that the amount of dark energy in the universe is actually increasing. See Rupert Sheldrake, *The Science Delusion: Freeing the Spirit of Enquiry*, 71.

[41] Ludwig Büchner, *Force and Matter* (New York: Peter Eckler, 1891), 10, 14, 21.

[42] Gerald Schroeder, *The Hidden Face of God* (New York: Touchstone, 2001), 186.

WHY IS THERE SOMETHING RATHER THAN NOTHING?

Any intellectually honest person will admit that he *does not* know *why the universe exists. Scientists, of course, readily admit their ignorance on this point.*[43]

—Sam Harris

Why is there something rather than nothing?[44]

—Gottfried Leibniz

Gottfried Leibniz, an eighteenth-century German philosopher, asked the question other philosophers have certainly pondered, *"Why is there something rather than nothing?"* The question itself makes sense and goes to the very core of existence. However, what doesn't make sense, is how modern atheists reject one of the few possible

---

[43]Sam Harris, *Letter to a Christian Nation* (New York: Vintage Books, 2008), 74.
[44]Gottfried Wilhelm Leibniz, *The Philosophical Works of Leibnitz* (New Haven, CT: Tuttle, Morehouse & Taylor Publishers, 1890), 213.

answers available while, at the same time, admitting scientists are ignorant on the subject.

Unlike ancient philosophers or even philosophers in the 1950s, we are no longer confronted with the possibility that the universe has always existed. That there was a beginning is generally accepted by deists, theists and atheists alike.

However, in seeking to understand and explain how the universe came into existence, it seems there are really only a few possible explanations available and for each of these there is an implied answer to the question, "*why?*" Logically, if the universe has not always existed, then it is either the result of a random accident, a necessity or a decision.

1. *An accident*—if the universe were an accident, there would be no real reason why the universe exists. However, for an accident to occur, there would still have to have been something to cause it and something from which the universe could have emerged. If there was nothing from which matter, space, energy, laws, life, purposeful information, time and consciousness could emerge, there could have been no accident. So, while theoretically conceivable, this doesn't seem plausible—*nothing can't cause something even by accident.*[45]
2. *A necessity*—Stephen Hawking used this approach in his *theory of everything.* However, as previously highlighted, this theory still requires something to exist—some law of nature and necessity—to make something out of nothing by necessity. Again, while theoretically conceivable, this doesn't seem remotely plausible to many other physicists and cosmologists. It isn't logical and has no evidence to support it—*nothing can't*

---

[45]See John Lennox, *God and Stephen Hawking: Whose Design Is It Anyway?* (Oxford, England: Lion Book, 2011).

dictate or require something to occur. But, if it did, the reason for its existence would have been circular and nonsensical—it exists because it made itself exist.

3. *A decision*—the last option available to us is that the universe exists because of a choice. If it doesn't exist because of an accident or because of a necessity, it could only exist because of a decision for it to exist. This scenario would require a decision-maker with the ability to bring physical matter, space, energy, laws, life, purposeful information, time and consciousness into existence from nothing (from the nonphysical).

Can any of these theories be definitely proven? They likely can't with the tools of science. After all, how can science prove what happened before the existence of matter, time and space?

However, to dismiss even the *possibility* that the universe came into existence by choice rather than by accident or necessity is to expose a bias and makes no sense. As one of only three options available, it is certainly no less plausible than the other two.

Paul Davies maintains that any search for the reason for the big bang *"must lie beyond science."*[46] Science is incapable of providing the answer. He also suggests that the scorn, which many scientists demonstrate toward the notion that God exists and is the reason for the universe, makes no sense:

> *There is no doubt that many scientists are opposed temperamentally to any form of metaphysical, let alone mystical arguments. They are scornful of the notion that there might exist a*

[46] Paul Davies, *The Mind of God* (New York: Simon and Schuster, 1992), 57.

> God, or even an impersonal creative principle or
> ground of being that would underpin reality and
> render its contingent aspects less starkly arbi-
> trary. Personally I do not share their scorn.
> Although many metaphysical and theistic theo-
> ries seem contrived or childish, they are not obvi-
> ously more absurd than the belief that the
> universe exists, and exists in the form it does,
> reasonlessly.[47]

Logically, Professor Davies seems to be correct.

---

[47]Paul Davies, *The Mind of God*, 231.

GOD

WE DENY GOD AND ACCOUNTABILITY

*The concept "God" has hitherto been the
greatest objection to human existence. . . . We
deny God; in denying God, we deny accountability; only by doing that do we redeem the
world.*[48]

—Friedrich Nietzsche

Friedrich Nietzsche voiced his denial of God as a declaration of independence. He denied the existence of God
and cast off the fetters of religion, religious institutions and
accountability. In doing so, he saw his denial as world
redeeming. He was free!

Nietzsche obviously had an authority problem. His
solution was to deny the existence of the being to which his
society saw as their ultimate accountability—God.
Nietzsche also had a morality problem. His solution was

---

[48] Friedrich Nietzsche, *Twilight of the Idols* and *The Antichrist*
(Middlesex, England; Penguin Books, 1969), 54.

to deny the authority of the institutions from which his society derived their morals—religion.

Nietzsche ultimately wanted to liberate the world from what he thought had made mankind tamed and weakened—belief in God and Christian morality. However, as we will see in a few chapters, Nietzsche didn't totally reject morality. His *"good"* was whatever made mankind more powerful; his *"evil"* was whatever came from weakness.[49]

Given this, he saw Christian morality and the idea that pity should be shown to the weak as detrimental to mankind.[50] To him, any morality that didn't **cause** the *"weak"* and the *"botched"* to perish was harmful.[51] He thought we should help natural selection to do its job.

There are many problems with Nietzsche's declaration of independence from God and his rejection of morality and accountability, but two are obvious:

1. *His denial doesn't make it so*—Just because we deny the existence of something or someone doesn't make it so. Try denying the existence of the Internal Revenue Service. It won't make your tax bill go away. In the same way, rather than arguing why he believed there is no God, Nietzsche merely declared it to be so.[52]

2. *Morality and accountability are needed*—Even most modern atheists would not agree that a moral code—where the strong survive and the weak are victimized—is a good thing. While they may confess that morality is paradoxical to natural selection, they usually say that some sort of moral code that helps the

---

[49]Friedrich Nietzsche, *The AntiChrist* (New York: Alfred A. Knopf, 1920), 42.

[50]Ibid., 43, 45, 47, 49.

[51]Ibid., 43.

[52]Without stating how, Nietzsche seems to have assumed that the Enlightenment had proven God's demise.

weak and accountability to moral standards are needed. Nietzsche's notion of being a "free spirit" without accountability just doesn't work in real life.

In a way, Nietzsche's denial of God resembles a child's tantrum—I can't do what I want, so I'll reject you. Whether he denied God to justify his rejection of Christian morality or his rejection of God came first is perhaps debatable. However, it's clear from his writings that he expended vastly more ink attacking Christian morality than he did asserting God's nonexistence.

It's sometimes difficult to understand people's motives in saying the things they do. Yet, in Nietzsche's case, his denial of God and his denial of accountability to Christian standards of morality seemed to be strongly linked. What doesn't make sense is that the kind of morality he embraced in its place was hardly moral.

I DON'T WANT
THERE TO BE A GOD

*I want atheism to be true and am made
uneasy by the fact that some of the most intelligent and well-informed people I know are
religious believers. It isn't just that I don't
believe in God and, naturally, hope that I'm
right in my belief. It's that I hope there is no
God! I don't want there to be a God; I don't
want the universe to be like that.*[53]

—Thomas Nagel

Thomas Nagel dispenses with the arguments, debate,
and emotional name-calling some people embrace and
makes an honest admission. He just says it. He doesn't
want God to exist.

Nagel diagnoses himself as having a *"cosmic authority
problem."*[54] He doesn't want there to be a God who created, owns and governs the universe. And to some degree,
this does make sense. We generally do want to make our

---

[53]Thomas Nagel, *The Last Word* (New York: Oxford University Press, 1997), 130.
[54]Ibid., 131.

own decisions, direct our own lives, define our own purpose and morality and be ultimately accountable to no one.
So if we see God as an obstacle, we might not want God to
exist. I get that. But is that how the universe really is? If it's
not, does it really make sense to long for a reality that
doesn't and can't exist?

A universe where we all individually define our own
purpose, truth, and morality makes no sense. If my purpose
or morality—the ones I choose—hurt you and others in
horrible ways and keep you from pursuing your desired
purpose and morality, are mine valid? Can opposing views
of purpose, morality and truth all be valid?

Logically, practically and historically, no. Otherwise,
we have no basis for saying people like Adolph Hitler are
evil or Mother Teresa was good. And, if the truth I choose
is valid regardless of whether it conflicts with yours, why
would anyone consider lying, false advertising and perjury
to be a problem? A self-centered universe makes no sense
in light of the universe that actually exists.

A group-centered universe makes no sense either. If it
did, any group, party, race, nation or sect would be justified in anything they did to anyone else. However, we
know the largest, smartest or most powerful group isn't
always truthful or in the right. That's also not the way the
universe is.

We, as individuals and groups, obviously make our
own choices, and these choices, while not unlimited or
always unharmful, are genuine. We aren't puppets. If God
does exist, he's not a puppet master or a dictator. We aren't
forced to recognize him, agree with him or follow him. So,
why have a "cosmic authority problem"? Perhaps it's the
notion that we can live the way we want without ultimate
consequences or accountability that we desire.

The idea of a "cosmic authority problem" makes even less sense if, in fact, the God of the universe is benevolent. If God does exist and is good, pure, just, faithful, truthful and loving, why would we not want to know that? Why would we want a God like that to not exist? It makes no sense—at least not to me.

I REFUSE TO BELIEVE IN A GOD WHO HIDES

If God were real he would show himself to the world. Instead, the Bible says that he is hiding. I refuse to believe in a God like that.

—Anonymous (paraphrased)

Several modern atheists cite a verse from the Bible that states God is hiding, as evidence the God of the Bible isn't real. The verse is from the Jewish prophet Isaiah and is found in the Old Testament (the *Tanakh*). It says, *"You are indeed a God who concealed Himself, O God of Israel, who bring victory!"*[55] They reason that, if God is real, he wouldn't hide—he would show himself to the world.

What they fail to mention is the number of instances recorded in the Hebrew Scriptures where God did reveal himself to people. In fact, the *Tanakh* presents itself as the

---

[55]Isaiah 45:15 The quotation provided is from the Jewish Publication Society translation (https://jps.org/). The NIV translation is very similar: *"Truly you are a God who hides himself, O God and Savior of Israel."*

narrative of God's centuries-long **interaction** with a group of people who ultimately became the nation of Israel. This history is punctuated with the appearances of God to the Jewish people.

The *Tanakh* records that God revealed himself to and interacted with people like Noah, Abraham, Isaac, Jacob, Moses, the entire nation of Israel, Joshua, and the prophets—Jonah, Samuel, Nathan, Elijah, Elisha, Isaiah, Ezekiel, Daniel, Jeremiah, Micah, Nahum, Zephaniah and Zechariah—to name a few.

He also gave them direction and responded to their requests. So, to cherry-pick a passage and characterize the God of the *Tanakh* as being in hiding isn't really a fair depiction of what it actually says. You might not agree with it, but at least characterize it accurately.

The question of whether God is hiding is a good one. We would likely all acknowledge that hearing a thunderous voice from heaven, seeing glorious visions and being transported to heaven and back are not within the realm of the average American's experience. However, the *Pew Research Center* found that 80 percent of American Christians, who attend church at least monthly, say they sense God's presence while they're there.[56]

Is what they're feeling real? They believe it is. Are these people delusional as Richard Dawkins might suggest? It's possible. However, it's also possible that these millions of people are not delusional and have actually experienced something from a God who is not in hiding—at least not from them.

---

[56] "Why Americans Go (and Don't Go) to Religious Services," (Washington, DC: Pew Research Center, August 1, 2018), http://www.pewforum.org/2018/08/01/why-americans-go-to-religious-services/

Is God hiding? In pondering this even from a purely human standpoint, why would you reveal yourself to someone who doesn't really want to know you? You might just introduce yourself so they can see you're real, kind and have their best interests at heart. But you also just might wait and interact with them when they want to know you. Perhaps it's the same with God. Perhaps he is more inclined to interact with those who want to know him. That would make sense.

THERE IS NO GOD

We are each free to believe what we want, and it's my view that the simplest explanation is that there is no God. No one created the universe and no one directs our fate.[57]

—Stephen Hawking

Stephen Hawking is correct when he said we can all choose to believe what we want. However, to say *"there is no God,"* while a simple statement, is also a bold one. It is infinitely bolder than to merely say, *"I don't believe in God."* To confidently say *"there is no God"* is to presume to have the knowledge only God could possess—omniscience—complete knowledge of everything!

Was Stephen Hawking able to peer behind the invisible curtain of the big bang or beyond time and matter to ascertain what may exist in dimensions unknown? Was he

---

[57]Stephen Hawking, *Brief Answers to the Big Questions* (New York: Bantam Books, 2018), 38.

omniscient? Even Richard Dawkins dared not make the bold statement that there is no God. He pulled up short and just said, *"there almost certainly is no God."*[58]

A friend of mine, when confronted with a man who made a similar pronouncement that there is no God, asked him a simple question. He asked, *"What is my dog's name?"* I stood silent as the man responded, *"What do you mean?"* He again asked, *"Do you know what my dog's name is?"* The man, a bit confused, said, *"No."* *"Well then,"* my friend said, *"it seems that there is valid knowledge beyond your personal experience. Perhaps that includes the knowledge of God."*

He made a good point.

---

[58]Richard Dawkins, *The God Delusion* (New York: Mariner Books, 2008), 137.

SCIENCE
DISPROVES GOD

... I will go much further and argue that by this moment in time science has advanced sufficiently to be able to make a definitive statement on the existence of a God having the attributes that are traditionally associated with the Judeo-Christian-Islamic God.[59]

—Victor Stenger

It's a relatively new argument to say that science disproves God. It used to be that atheists contended the existence of God couldn't be proven. So to say a definitive answer is possible—that God's existence has been disproven—is a big leap. What's the logic behind the leap?

A lack of gaps disproves God—One of Victor Stenger's contentions was that theists must prove the universe can't exist without a God:

---

[59]Victor Stenger, God: *The Failed Hypothesis* (Amherst, NY: Prometheus Books, 2007), 11.

. . . if God exists, he must appear somewhere within the gaps or errors of scientific models.[60]

This is the atheist version of the *God of the gaps* approach—if you can't explain something, then God must have done it. This isn't a reliable approach for theists or atheists because a God may have chosen to use natural means to accomplish the objective of bringing forth life in the universe. It may be there are no "gaps" but that doesn't disprove God.

However, in response to Stenger, there actually are a huge number of gaps and "chicken or the egg scenarios" that science can't currently answer. Fazale Rana, a biochemist, has highlighted many of them related to cells. Let's look at just a few:

- **DNA *and proteins**—Rana points out that *"proteins can't be produced without DNA, and DNA can't be produced without proteins." "DNA can't replicate on its own."*[61] Since DNA and proteins are both needed for life to exist, how could they have come into existence simultaneously? Scientists don't know.[62]
- *Proteins make other proteins*—The process in the cell that makes proteins from amino acids requires the same proteins that it makes to make proteins.[63] How then, did this circular process get started?
- *Minimum genome size*—Life needs more than just a few genes to exist. Rana points out, *"the simplest*

[60]Ibid., 13.
[61]Fazale Rana, *The Cell's Design* (Grand Rapids: Baker Books, 2008), 99, 101.
[62]Stephen Meyer points out that protein-first, DNA-first and RNA-first models to explain the emergence of life have all failed. See Stephen Meyer, *Signature in the Cell* (New York, NY: HarperOne, 2009), 322.
[63]Rana, *The Cell's Design*, 105.

life-forms capable of independent living require roughly 1,300 and 2,300 gene products" and even parasitic microbes, which can't live without a host life form, require hundreds of gene products. And, this genetic information must be organized and stored in a specific location for them to exist.[64] How then, did life get started? We don't yet know.

- *Specific genes are required*—Not only is a lot of genetic information required for life to exist, genes controlling five processes must simultaneously exist for a reproducing cell to live. They all had to be present in the first living cell, and science can't explain how it happened.

    . . . life in its bare minimum form requires genes that control DNA replication, cell division, protein synthesis and assembly of the cell membrane. Minimal life also depends upon genes that specify at least one biochemical pathway that can extract energy from the environment.[65]

While Fazale Rana highlights that science can't answer these gaps in knowledge, his contention is not that science may not be able to answer some of them in the future. His primary point seems to be that the way cells operate demonstrates interdependent integrated components and processes, including quality control, requiring a large amount of coded information, a significant level of simultaneously coordinated development and optimization that would be highly consistent with an architect or a designer.

---

[64]Ibid., 57, 66.
[65]Ibid., 62.

A workable theory disproves God—Victor Stenger also advanced the idea that if a scientific theory can be developed which explains the existence of our universe, then no miracle of creation is required and science disproves God.[66] He then pointed to Stephen Hawking's assertion that the negative energy of gravity counteracts the positive energy of matter in the universe thus making the total energy of the universe equal to zero. Since the total is zero they equal nothing and no miracle was required! However, this notion is flawed.

It's clear that there are far more than just two things in the universe. There is matter, gravity, space, time, purposeful information, life, consciousness, laws and possibly things of which we are still unaware. However, even if there were only two things that inversely equaled each other, there are still two variables and an equation that sums to zero. The two variables (things) exist. Something would still have to cause the existence of these two things to emerge from nothingness. And, as other scientists and mathematicians have pointed out, the notion that this could have occurred is merely a philosophical speculation. It's not a workable theory.

Is the idea that science can't disprove God just a theistic cop-out? Is it just a way of ducking the question? Not really. Scientists have long observed that science has its limitations and its ability to opine on God's existence is one of them. For example, the late Stephen Jay Gould, an evolutionary biologist and a Harvard and NYU professor, maintained that science can't actually disprove God.

---

[66]Stenger, *God: The Failed Hypothesis*, 116–17.

. . . science can work only with naturalistic expla-
nations; it can neither affirm nor deny other types
of actors (like God) in other spheres (the moral
realm, for example.)[67]

Though science likely can't prove or disprove God, is the existence of God fundamentally inconsistent with science? Many scientists say the answer is, no. In fact, it's actually compatible with what science has uncovered.

Freeman Dyson, a physicist and member of the team that developed the first nuclear bomb, does not claim there is a God or that God created the universe. He does however, state that the idea that mind (intelligence) is behind the operation of the universe is consistent with the architecture of the universe:

. . . I do not claim that the architecture of the
universe proves the existence of God. I claim only
that the architecture of the universe is consistent
with the hypothesis that mind plays an essential
role in its functioning.[68]

So, while some scientists assert that science has disproven the existence of God, it seems this is simply not the case. Scientific discoveries about the way life operates and the intelligence that's evident in the universe are actually consistent with the idea that life and the universe were designed.

---

[67] Francis Collins, *The Language of God* (New York: Free Press, 2007), 166.
[68] Freeman Dyson, *Disturbing the Universe* (New York: Basic Books, 1979), 251.

WHAT ABOUT EPICURUS' PARADOX?

Epicurus was an ancient Greek philosopher who lived from about 341 to 270 BC. His general philosophy was that pleasure is good, pain is evil and life should be lived to maximize peaceful enjoyment. He was not an extreme hedonist, saw mankind as being able to influence their own fates and saw human sensation ending at the point of death. And, now you are probably wondering why any of this is relevant.

It's relevant because Epicurus' Paradox, as recorded by Lactantius,[69] is still one of the more commonly cited "proofs" for the nonexistence of God. David Hume, a leading philosopher in the eighteenth century, summarized the paradox as follows:

> *Epicurus's old questions are yet unanswered. Is he [God] willing to prevent evil, but not able? Then is he impotent. Is he able, but not willing? Then is he malevolent. Is he both able and willing? Whence then is evil?*[70]

---

[69]Lactantius was an early fourth-century Roman educator and historian. He was also the tutor of Crispus, one of Emperor Constantine's four sons.
[70]David Hume, *Dialogues Concerning Natural Religion* (London: 1779), 186.

The number of times the Epicurean Paradox has been used to assert the nonexistence of God is astonishing. It's astonishing because *Epicurus wasn't an atheist*; he actually did believe in God. In fact, he believed there were many gods and instructed others to believe in them as well:

> *First of all believe that god is a being immortal and blessed, even as the common idea of a god is engraved on men's minds, and do not assign to him anything alien to his immortality or ill-suited to his blessedness; but believe about him everything that can uphold his blessedness and immortality. For gods there are, since the knowledge of them is by clear vision.*[71]

—Epicurus, *Epicurus to Menoeceus*

Epicurus believed in the gods of ancient Greece. He simply asserted that God didn't actively intervene in the affairs of mankind and our futures aren't subject to destiny.[72]

Even if the Epicurean Paradox was intended to assert the nonexistence of God, which it wasn't, it fails as a "proof." It fails because it focuses on only two attributes—one moral attribute (goodness) and one metaphysical attribute (ability).

Even theists would agree a two-attribute god doesn't exist. Theists contend that God possesses multiple moral attributes (truthfulness, goodness, faithfulness, purity, justice and love) and multiple metaphysical attributes. The latter would usually include the ideas that God is eternal, spirit, all-powerful, all-knowing, and all-present.

---

[71]Epicurus, *Epicurus to Menoeceus*, Cyril Bailey, trans., *Epicurus, The Extant Remains* (Oxford, England: Clarendon Press, 1926), 83.
[72]*Epicurus, The Extant Remains* (Oxford, England: Clarendon Press, 1926), 135.

Instead of asking the Epicurean Paradox, it may be more relevant to ask a broader question—if there is a God, why does he allow pain and suffering in the world? More on that in the next chapter—

THE PROBLEM
OF PAIN

In the language of science, the empirical fact of unnecessary suffering in the world is inconsistent with a god who is omniscient, omnipotent, and omnibenevolent.[73]

—Victor Stenger

Does the existence of pain and suffering in the world disprove the existence of a knowing, powerful and good God? Would a God like that allow or possibly even design pain into the universe? It seems like the answer depends on what the objective was for creating the universe and the people in it. If the objective was for everyone to be comfortable and happy, the answer is no. However, if pain is a tool or a by-product rather than the objective, the answer could be yes.

---

[73]Victor Stenger, *God: The Failed Hypothesis* (Amherst, NY: Prometheus Books, 2007), 214.

THE FREEDOM TO FAIL

Let's start by looking at people. People aren't puppets. We have the freedom to make good and bad choices. We can be wise or foolish. We can be selfish or generous. We can be kind or mean. We can even rescue or kill. **Freedom** is important. Without it, you wouldn't really be you. You would be like a puppet on a string.

Given this, it isn't difficult to see why a **loving** God would grant us genuine choices. Without genuine choice, love isn't love, gifts aren't gifts, and friendship isn't friendship. Without genuine choice, these things are merely programmed responses. Perhaps a God who wanted us to have the genuine capacity to love would give us the freedom to make genuine choices and, with it, the freedom to fail. If that's the case, pain is allowed to achieve the ultimate objective of creating free, relational, independent beings.[74]

THE PARENT ANALOGY

To assert that the existence of pain and suffering in the world proves God doesn't exist is sort of like saying it proves parents don't exist. As parents, we don't want our children to suffer. However, as parents, there are bigger goals to consider than our children's momentary pleasure and comfort. We want them to become mature, wise, compassionate, responsible and creative adults. When we look at the bigger objective, we realize not all pain and suffering is bad—sometimes it's a tool. Here are a few examples:

- *Consequences*—When kids make decisions and choices, they ultimately encounter consequences. To

---

[74]Since created beings would be ultimately be dependent upon God for existence, their independence would not be unlimited.

insulate our children from all of the consequences of their decisions is to insulate them from reality and deny them the **wisdom** and **motivation** that consequences provide. So, we let them feel the pain.

- *Challenges*—Parents allow their kids to play competitive sports, even though they can get hurt. Climbing mountains can be painful too. They're painful but the enjoyment from the challenge is greater than the dread of the pain. After all, what would life be like without challenges and adventure?
- *Compassion*—Parents know problems create compassion. Children become more compassionate, protective and patient when they or their loved ones experience pain and adversity. We don't enjoy the pain but the fruit of it is compassion for others.
- *Creativity*—Need and scarcity fuel creativity; problems require solutions. Builders, mathematicians, engineers, doctors and artists blossom when problems need to be solved, and we and our society gain from their endeavors.
- *Humility and relationships*—Need causes us to see that we don't have everything under control and we need other people. We might even need God. Our need helps facilitate relationships, teamwork and friendships.

The bottom line to all this is, parents know not all pain and problems are bad for our children. In fact, parents intentionally intervene in their children's lives in ways children often find to be painful. Even extremely loving, powerful, wealthy and highly educated parents do this. They do it all the time. Why?

- *To Equip*—Parents send their kids to school, make them do their chores and insist that they practice the trumpet. This preparation and work can be difficult. It's not fun. However, the short-term inconvenience is paled by the long-term reward. It prepares them for life.

- *To Discipline*—Whether your parenting philosophy includes time-outs, spankings, adjustments in privileges or a combination thereof, loving discipline is good for children. Though children may not enjoy it, parents love them enough to temporarily make them miserable so they won't grow up to be spoiled or hurtful adults.

Okay, now back to the question of whether pain and suffering in the world disproves the existence of God. Does it? It obviously doesn't disprove the existence of parents, who are generally loving though finite beings. If there is a God, it seems that he also could have good reasons for allowing us to experience hardships.

WHAT ABOUT EXTREME PAIN AND EVIL?

The parent analogy is easy to understand. Now what about **big pain and big suffering**—holocausts, tsunamis, world wars and the like? This is the kind of pain and suffering Victor Stenger would likely deem to be *"unnecessary."* Would a good and powerful God not intervene in situations like this? Perhaps not.

- *Natural disasters*—If God were to continually intervene in the natural order, there wouldn't be one. If the laws of nature weren't reliable, the effect on our ability to live could be worse than the occurrence of storms and earthquakes. Besides, most of us know living near a fault line or a volcano can be a bad idea.

- *Crime, wars and genocide*—If God took away our ability to do evil, we would also no longer have the **freedom** to do good. Unfortunately, people do choose to do evil. That's not God's fault. Theologians say that the most loving way for God to have made us was to make us free.[75] Otherwise, we wouldn't really be human **beings**. We would be preprogrammed human-looking machines.
- *Disease*—A few years ago, a wealthy hedge fund manager gave $100 million to help find a cure for a rare blood disease afflicting his daughter. His love for his daughter spilled over into the lives of other people going through the same plight. Would he have been that compassionate and giving had his daughter not been suffering? I don't know. But if this is the fruit of suffering, it's logical God would allow it.

IS THIS THE BEST POSSIBLE WORLD?

Some people ask, if God is real, is this the best world he could possibly have made? Could he not have made people who wanted to do good all the time? Yes, but they would be programmed and not really free. Could he not have made a world without hurricanes and tornados? Yes, but without prevailing winds and pressure systems, the world wouldn't cool properly. Could he not have made people healthy all the time? Yes, but the compassion that results from sickness may make the world a better place than without it. Is this really the best he could do? Perhaps.

---

[75]Various religions state that, though God has provided moral precepts for us to follow, we still choose to disregard them. Christianity further teaches that God entered the world to: 1) demonstrate how we should live, 2) atone for our moral failures and 3) provide us with help (through his indwelling presence) in how to live morally.

The answer depends on what God's objective was in making the world and populating it with life. If his objective was to make a problem-free world, then it seems he could have done a better job. However, if his objective was to create intelligent, conscious, relational people who have genuine choices, and a world for them to live in that fosters their growth and choices to love, create, assume responsibility, and be moral, then it seems he did a really good job. Besides, maybe he has more things planned for the future.

WILL THERE BE A FUTURE STATE?

The Scriptures of the three big monotheistic faiths state that God allows evil, but that there will be a future state of heaven and a new earth where evil is no longer present. This is obviously too big a subject for us to explore here— it could fill several books. However, a future state where those who have chosen to do evil are separated from those who have responded to God and received his forgiveness, would be a pretty cool place for the forgiven. In this future state, those who have chosen to follow God would be helped by God to live morally.

So, why wouldn't God just skip to the future state and avoid all the pain and suffering? It's possible that the messiness of choice is needed for us to freely choose to respond to God.

DOES PAIN AND SUFFERING
DISPROVE GOD?

Antony Flew, once one of the world's most vocal atheists, long pondered this question of pain, suffering and evil. This was the big issue that caused him to become an atheist in the first place. However, fifty years later, his conclusion was that *"the existence of God does not depend on the existence of warranted or unwarranted evil."*[76] In other words, the fact that extreme pain and suffering exists in the world doesn't prove or disprove the existence of God.

So, where does that leave us? It seems a good God could have good reasons for allowing pain and suffering to exist. Given this, the existence of pain and suffering in the world doesn't disprove God. Claiming it does, doesn't really make sense.

[76]Antony Flew, *There Is a God* (New York: HarperCollins, 2007), 156.

MEANING, MORALITY AND PURPOSE

THERE IS NO REASON TO LIVE

Introspection can't provide a good reason to go on living because there isn't any. This is the one thing that existentialists got right. But introspection keeps hoping, looking, trying to find a reason to go on. Since there really isn't one, those who look hard eventually become troubled.[77]

—Alex Rosenberg

Alex Rosenberg, former chair of the philosophy department at Duke University, sees no purpose to the universe, no meaning to life and no real reason to live. To him, we exist purely by *"dumb luck."* In his view of the world, you are born for no reason, live for no reason and die for no reason. He says any reason you think you may have to live is merely an illusion of your own mind's making.[78]

---

[77]Alex Rosenberg, *The Atheist's Guide to Reality* (New York: W. W. Norton & Company, 2011), 280.
[78]Ibid., 205.

Rosenberg's view is that reality is what physics says it is and physics has no meaning, values, rights, morals or purpose.[79] It's just physics. So, if you're taking his philosophy class at Duke, just keep in mind that whether you attend class, graduate or even win another NCAA championship in basketball doesn't really matter, because physics doesn't care what you do.

Hmmm. Why does this philosophy (**nihilism**), not seem to fit with the reality of our daily lives? It's probably because to you and to billions of other people, you do have purpose and a reason to live. So, is everyone delusional? Are our reasons to go on living just shared fantasies? It seems to Alex Rosenberg, the answer is yes.

> *Whatever is in our brain driving our lives from cradle to grave, it is not purpose. But it does produce the powerful illusion of purpose, just like all the other purposeless adaptations in the biological realm.*[80]
>
> —Alex Rosenberg

Why then should we go on living? Rosenberg certainly doesn't advocate suicide or self-harm. Instead, he says we can **enjoy** a purposeless life. He also suggests that being moral (according to commonly evolved "*core morality*") feels better than not being moral.[81]

What Alex Rosenberg is essentially proposing is that we invent our own **reason** to live based on the objective of **feeling good**. What he implicitly acknowledges is that we all **need** a reason to live that is more compelling than not

---

[79]Ibid., 2–3, 279, 288, 296.
[80]Ibid., 205.
[81]Ibid., 3, 283, 313.

living. Life, in order to be lived, requires a reason[82]—since he says physics can't provide it, he proposes one of his own. Kai Nielsen, another atheist philosopher, doesn't agree with Rosenberg's view of life. He thinks things do matter. Though not directing this comment at Alex Rosenberg, Nielsen said:

> A man who says, 'If God is dead, nothing matters,' is a spoilt child who has never looked at his fellow man with compassion.[83]

Who is correct, Mr. Rosenberg or Mr. Nielsen? Is physics really the only legitimate source of meaning, value, rights, morality and purpose? Are we all living an illusion that these things even exist? If there is no real reason to live and if no reason is needed, why does Rosenberg suggest a purpose of his own—pleasure—to fill the void?

Alex Rosenberg acknowledges that his views may be troubling. For those who find nihilism with a meaningless and purposeless life of no intrinsic value to be depressing, he suggests you *"take a Prozac or your favorite serotonin reuptake inhibitor, and keep taking them till they kick in."*[84]

That's one approach.

---

[82]Even simple self-continuation is a reason.
[83]Kai Nielsen, *Ethics without God* (Amherst, NY: Prometheus Books, 1990), 227–28.
[84]Ibid., 315.

THERE IS NO RIGHT
OR WRONG

*What is the difference between right and
wrong, good and bad? There is no difference
between them.*[85]

—Alex Rosenberg

A few years ago, one of my daughter's high school class-mates strongly declared to her, *"There is no such thing
as right or wrong."* The girl was from Asia, and she and
her family didn't believe in God. To her way of thinking,
if there is no God and people are merely the product of the
laws of nature, the idea of morality makes no sense.

My daughter, a rather insightful young lady, quickly
responded with the question, *"Then it's okay to murder
someone?"* The girl replied, *"Oh, no, you shouldn't murder."* *"But, if there is no right or wrong,"* my daughter said,
*"it doesn't make sense to say that you shouldn't do some-
thing. You can do whatever you want."* The girl made no
rebuttal but was still unconvinced. Yet my daughter made

---

[85]Alex Rosenberg, *The Atheist's Guide to Reality* (New York: W. W. Norton & Co.,
2011), 3.

a great point. The very idea that you should or shouldn't do something is a moral judgment about what is right or wrong.

Most American atheists wouldn't agree with the notion that there is no such thing as right or wrong. Even if they reject the idea of moral absolutes, they generally value some form of morality. Without morality, society would be a dangerous mess—the survival of the fittest can get really ugly.

Yet two questions remain—what kind of moral code is truly moral, and is a God required for that kind of morality to exist?

WORTH IS BASED ON USEFULNESS

*Every elevation of the type "man," has hith-
erto been the work of an aristocratic society—
and so will it always be—a society believing
in a long scale of gradations of rank and differences in worth among human beings, and
requiring slavery in some form or other.*[86]

—Friedrich Nietzsche

Friedrich Nietzsche was an interesting guy. Though an
atheist himself, he was the son of a Lutheran minister
who died when Friedrich was only five years old. He was
a leading cultural critic and philosopher in the late 1800s
and early 1900s. He's the man who coined the phrase
"God is dead."[87]

---

[86]Friedrich Nietzsche, *Beyond Good and Evil* (New York: MacMillan Company,
1907), 223.
[87]Friedrich Nietzsche, *Joyful Wisdom* (New York: Frederick Unger Publishing,
1960), 225.

For a time, he was a good friend of the composer Richard Wagner. And, based on his letters, seems to have been gracious to his family and friends. However, many of his ideas and the brute force with which he expressed them were really harsh and were not embraced by most Europeans. Nietzsche held tightly to the idea that natural selection was imbued with a morality—the betterment of the human race—that was humanity's duty to uphold. He saw invalids as having no right to live, pity as being a violation of natural selection, the Christian idea of the equality of souls to be a destructive falsehood and Christians and Polish Jews to be repugnant.[88] To many of us, his form of morality would seem immoral.

At the core of Nietzsche's morality were at least three key assumptions: 1) there is no ultimate accountability to God, 2) human worth is based upon usefulness, and 3) restrictions imposed by religion are wrong.

IS HUMAN WORTH BASED ON USEFULNESS?

The problem with Nietzsche's morality is that it's extended to people based upon their **rank in society**—to him people don't possess equal value or worth. He saw the exploitation of others as "*a primary organic function*;" it wasn't "*depraved or imperfect*;" it was part of the natural order.[89] He saw oppression as improving mankind.

Nietzsche's brand of morality actually justifies immorality. Morality that isn't universally applied, even to the non-productive or to other races, isn't moral in the eyes of

---

[88]Friedrich Nietzsche, *Twilight of the Idols* and *The Antichrist*, (Middlesex, England: Penguin Books, 1969), 88, 118, 161, 186.
[89]Friedrich Nietzsche, *Beyond Good and Evil* (New York: MacMillan Company, 1907), 226–27.

those to whom it's denied. This is the sort of morality Adolph Hitler embraced—and that story didn't end well. Does atheism always result in views of human worth and morality as distorted as Nietzsche's? Not necessarily. However, many who embraced naturalism in the late 1800s and early 1900s shared Nietzsche's views. Many were scientists and university professors. For example, Alexander Tille, a German university professor and admirer of Nietzsche, stated:

> *From the doctrine that all men are children of God and equal before him, the ideal of humanitarianism and socialism has grown, that all humans have the same right to exist and the same value, and this ideal has greatly influenced behaviour in the last two centuries. This ideal is irreconcilable with the theory of evolution . . .*[90]
>
> *Zarathustra [Nietzshe] preaches: Do not spare your neighbor! For the person of today is something that must be overcome. But if it must be overcome, then the worst people, the low ones, and the superfluous ones must be sacrificed . . .*[91]

Ernst Haeckel, another early twentieth-century German university professor and atheist, saw the level of **intellect** as an appropriate measure of human value. Using this measure, he concluded:

> *These lower races (such as the Veddahs or Australian negroes) are psychologically nearer to the mammals (apes or dogs) than to civilized*

---

[90]Richard Weikart, *From Darwin to Hitler*, (New York: Palgrave MacMillan, 2004), 94.
[91]Ibid., 45.

Europeans; we must, therefore, assign a totally different value to their lives.[92]

Hopefully, we would all conclude that selectively applied morality isn't really moral.

WHAT DO MODERN ATHEISTS SAY?

Fortunately, most leading atheists today have embraced moral codes that are higher than Nietzsche's and Haeckel's. They don't advocate slavery or the subjugation of "inferior" peoples. But the same moral questions persist. Is morality and our right to be treated morally determined by naturalism—is it about the survival of the fittest or even the survival of the group? And, if we can't contribute to society in a meaningful way or live a life of a certain quality, do we necessarily even have a right to live? Some say no.

Obviously, since the new ethical outlook I have been defending rejects even the view that all human lives are of equal worth, I am not going to hold that all life is of equal worth, irrespective of its quality or characteristics.[93]

—Peter Singer

Peter Singer says all human life doesn't have equal value. In doing so, he travels down the same perilously slippery slope as Nietzsche. He maintains that the severely handicapped, the unborn, and even the newborn don't have the same right to live as those who are healthy.

---

[92]Ernst Haeckel, *The Wonders of Life* (London, England: Watts & Co., 1904), 406.
[93]Peter Singer, *Rethinking Life and Death* (New York: St. Martin's Griffin, 1994), 202–3.

Mr. Singer might even allow parents of newborn babies twenty-eight days to decide whether to keep a child or have it killed.[94] Allowing a physically nonviable life to die is one thing, but granting parents a month to decide if they want a child with Down syndrome to live or die is quite another. It's a very slippery slope indeed—one Nietzsche boldly traveled.

While enduring the crippling effects of ALS, would Stephen Hawking have had no value as a human being without his computer as a means of communicating? Was his worth based only on his usefulness? Had he no value as a person?

Natural selection says that the strongest will survive but morality says the strong **should** help the weak. This is because the true foundation of morality is the inherent value of every person—regardless of their race, religion, nationality or physical handicap. If people don't have value, the only reason to help the weak, sick or poor is if it somehow benefits you or the greater good. However, the "greater good" can also be, and has been, used as a reason to justify incredible cruelty.

A view that people are merely the result of random natural processes has difficulty in justifying why the strong **should** help the weak, the healthy **should** care for the sick or the wealthy **should** provide for the poor. After all, who has the authority to ascribe worth to people? Theists say it's God and that all people have value.

---

[94]Ibid., 217.

WAIT A MINUTE, PEOPLE DO HAVE VALUE!

I conclude that, while it is true that science cannot decide questions of value, that is because they cannot be intellectually decided at all, and lie outside the realm of truth and falsehood.[95]

—Bertrand Russell

Bertrand Russell saw questions of value as falling in the realm of emotion rather than that of truth or falsehood. That's because to him, science doesn't ascribe value to anything—things just are. If Russell was correct that it's impossible to reach an intellectual decision about value, the basis for morality as we know it is gone. After all, morality assumes that people do have worth—people really are important.

---

[95]Bertrand Russell, *Religion and Science* (New York: Oxford University Press, 1997), 243.

If we determine a person's worth only based on what science can convey, we might reach one of two conclusions:

1. **People have no absolute value**—Bertrand Russell and other nihilists reached this conclusion.[96] To them, value is a foreign concept to science and, therefore, merely an emotional response. It's a concept with no basis in either truth or falsehood. Perhaps this is what caused Alex Rosenberg, another nihilist, to conclude *"scientism assures us that no one has any moral rights."*[97] Fortunately, the U.S. Declaration of Independence doesn't agree.

2. **Natural selection determines value**—If human worth is based only on what science conveys, the other option is that human value is based on the degree to which the species is advanced or how useful a person is. Friedrich Nietzsche and Adolph Hitler held to this view. There are several variations of this idea—the fittest, the most powerful, the richest, the most beautiful, the most productive or the smartest have the most value. If you see yourself at the top of the food chain, this might be attractive. Otherwise, not so much.

Many atheist scientists and philosophers have concluded these two positions can be really unhealthy for the human race. Instead, they've embraced a third position called **atheistic humanism**.[98] They conclude that while physics, chemistry, and biology can't ascribe value to people, people really are important.

---

[96] Bertrand Russell said that *"It is we who create value and our desires which confer value"* (*Why I Am Not a Christian*, p. 55).

[97] Alex Rosenberg, *The Atheist's Guide to Reality* (New York: W. W. Norton & Co., 2011), 296.

[98] It's also called secular humanism.

3. *People have value, because we say they do*—Atheistic humanism is the view that people do not have value because God said so, because they don't believe in God. They also don't believe that people have value because science says so because, to biology, a cell is just a cell. Instead, they ascribe value to people because they want people to have value. They see human value and morality that's based on the equal value of each person as important to human survival.[99]

In the *Humanist Manifesto 2000*, 141 prominent atheists agree that "*the dignity and autonomy of the individual is the central value.*"[100] They state that the virtues of empathy and caring are essential and that we have responsibilities to others.[101] They reject both God and nihilism, but they embrace the idea of human value and the need for morality.

The challenges of the first two approaches to human value are obvious—they can and have resulted in incredible pain and suffering. The third approach is much more beneficial to the human race, but it also has challenges. The most obvious is, if humans do have value, is it because a group of only 141 people say they do?

What if these people later change their minds? After all, there have been multiple versions of *Humanist Manifestos* over the years. They were drafted by different groups and signed by different people and the manifestos keep changing.[102] If, on the other hand, all people have inherent value without others having to say so, how did they get it?

---

[99]Paul Kurtz, *Humanist Manifesto 2000* (Amherst, NY: Prometheus Press, 2000), 35, 45–46.

[100]Ibid., 31.

[101]Ibid., 32.

[102]The *Humanist Manifesto I* was published in 1933 with thirty-four signers. *Humanist Manifesto II* was published in 1973. There was also a *Secular Humanist Declaration* in 1980 and a Declaration of Interdependence in 1988. The *Humanist*

The fact is, people do see value in themselves and in those they love. People also ascribe value to others, whom they don't even know and to things. For value to exist, **there must be someone who values.** There can't be value without a "valuer."

Otherwise, things just exist; they have no value—they just are. Yet, for people to genuinely have value and for that value to be equal, universal and unchangeable, there has to be one source to universally and equally ascribe it who doesn't waver in the decision. Theists say this one source can only be God.

Atheistic humanism has another challenge. Its moral code is substantially borrowed. Humanism is seen by many as atheism with morality borrowed from Christianity. Rupert Sheldrake says, to make up for the void in meaning, purpose and human value resulting from mechanistic science, atheists borrowed Christian morality.[103]

Even Michael Onfray, the author of *Atheist Manifesto*, seems to agree. He calls the mixing of atheism with Christian values "*Christian Atheism.*"[104] He proposes a new atheist morality that rejects Christian values.[105] However, what would that new moral code really resemble? Atheists from Bertrand Russell[106] to Richard Dawkins[107] have

---

Manifesto 2000 states "*It is not possible to create a permanent Manifesto, but it is useful and wise to devise a working document, open to revision*" (p. 8).

[103] Rupert Sheldrake, *The Science Delusion* (London: Hodder & Stoughton Ltd., 2013), 24–25.

[104] Michael Onfray, *Atheist Manifesto* (New York: Arcade Publishing, 2011), 55–57.

[105] Michael Onfray seems to propose a "*hedonist contract*" with society that's based on **utilitarianism** as advanced by Jeremy Bentham and John Stuart Mill (*Atheist Manifesto*, p. 58). However, a key problem with utilitarianism is that it can justify the oppression of a minority, if it results in greater happiness for the whole.

[106] Bertrand Russell, *Why I Am Not a Christian* (New York: Simon & Schuster, 1957), 5, 14–15.

[107] Richard Dawkins, *Atheists for Jesus*, https://www.rationalresponders.com/atheists _for_jesus_a_richard_dawkins_essay

expressed admiration for the moral code taught by Jesus of Nazareth. With what would they replace it?

So, it seems there are two big challenges for many atheists. The first is, the most logical way that all people could truly have equal value that never changes is if there is one unchangeable source who ascribes it. The second is, while they point to science as their authority for the nonexistence of God, they can't point to science as their source for human value, morality, meaning or purpose.

To science, there is none. Instead, they borrow their ideas of universal human value and the need to extend morality to others from those who do believe in God.

Am I alone, or does this seem a bit odd?

GOD ISN'T REQUIRED FOR MORALITY TO EXIST

. . . the existence of ethics can be explained as the product of evolution among long-lived social animals with the capacity to reason. Hence, the need for belief in laws of ethics existing independently of us disappears.[108]

The rules of ethics are not moral absolutes or unchallengeable intuitions. . . . In some unusual situations we should break ethical rules; but we do so at our own peril. Essential ethical rules must be publicly supported, and censuring those who break them is an important way of supporting them. . . . Though ethical rules have no ultimate authority of their own, there are some ethical rules we cannot do without.[109]

—Peter Singer

---

[108]Peter Singer, *The Expanding Circle: Ethics, Evolution and Moral Progress* (Princeton, NJ: Princeton University Press, 2011), 106.
[109]Ibid., 167.

Peter Singer, an atheist philosopher and Australian university professor, contends that morality and ethical rules do not depend on the existence of God. He sees them as the result of human evolution. He says, while there is no such thing as absolute right or wrong, we **should** have ethical rules because we need them. He also says that, at times, we should break the rules. If Singer is correct, why doesn't this seem like a very satisfying description of morality?

Can people be good if God doesn't exist? It's obvious that everyone—theists, deists, atheists and agnostics—can do good and evil things. It also seems obvious that pretty much everyone is morally aware—we have some sense of a moral code and make moral judgments. So morality exists. But what kind of morality exists and what kind is necessary for God to exist?

- *Naturalism is its own morality*—As has been already discussed, the idea that naturalism is its own morality gained traction in the late 1800s. This is the idea that the advancement of the species is the objective of nature and whatever helps to achieve that goal is moral. This moral code says the strong **should** survive and the weak **should** not.
- *Individual Subjectivism*—To say that what is moral is determined by each individual is the equivalent of saying morality doesn't exist. If everything you choose to do is moral, regardless of the effect on others or whether they agree with your definition of morality, the entire notion of right and wrong is meaningless—just do whatever you want.
- *Group Subjectivism*[110]—Like Peter Singer, Richard Dawkins attributes the existence of morality to

---

[110]Group subjectivism is also known as cultural relativism.

evolution. He sees moral awareness and moral codes as the result of a changing group *zeitgeist* evolving over time. In other words, he sees morality as being defined by a group of people (a culture) that changes as the culture does; it's group subjectivism.[111]

This kind of group-centered moral approach was used by the Nazis to enslave and kill millions of people. It benefited the Third Reich but was terrible for everyone else. It was also used by European nations and even America to justify colonialism and slavery. Yet, is a moral code that doesn't seek to be moral to everyone truly moral?

- *Objective morality*—Moral objectivism is the idea that what is right and wrong is *always* right and wrong for *everyone* and everyone should be treated that way.[112] It's not so much a list of rules as it is a set of moral principles that you follow in any given situation. Moral behavior is **truthful, faithful, just, good, pure,** and **loving** to everyone. And these principles don't conflict with each other—for example, being truthful or just doesn't require you to be unfaithful, impure or unloving. This is the highest possible moral code (at least for mere mortals) because it seeks the well-being of everyone.[113]

Obviously, the first two types of moral codes don't require the existence of God. Under them, people decide what's moral and that's close enough. However, an objective moral code based on non-conflicting moral

---

[111]Richard Dawkins, *The God Delusion* (New York: Mariner Books, 2008), 300–306.

[112]Objective morality should not be confused with Objectivism as proposed by Ayn Rand.

[113]This is not to be confused with Utilitarianism as espoused by Jeremy Bentham and John Stuart Mill.

principles and extended to everyone is a different story. This fits into the category of *moral law*—sort of like the laws of nature.

Does objective morality that approaches the level of universal moral law really exist and, if so, what is its source? The idea of objective moral law isn't new. Cicero, a first-century BC Roman lawyer, statesman and philosopher, observed that the laws of nations weren't always moral. He maintained that there was an eternal universal moral law higher than national law and that God was its source.[114] Was he correct?

Could *objective moral law* exist without the existence of God? Perhaps. However, it's questionable as to whether **non-conflicting** universal moral standards could. Like interdependent fine-tuned laws of nature, a set of non-conflicting moral principles that are universally beneficial would be consistent with the existence of God. However, this kind of morality does not seem to be the product of naturalism.

[114]Cicero, *The Republic and The Laws* (Oxford, England: Oxford University Press, 2008), 111, 124–25.

GOD IS NOT REQUIRED FOR MEANING AND PURPOSE TO EXIST

The more the universe seems comprehensible, the more it also seems pointless. . . . The effort to understand the universe is one of the very few things that lifts human life a little above the level of farce, and gives it some of the grace of tragedy.[115]

—Steven Weinberg

So far as scientific evidence goes, the universe has crawled by slow stages to a somewhat pitiful result on this earth and is going to crawl by still more pitiful stages to a condition of universal death. If this is to be taken as evidence of purpose, I can only say that the purpose is one that does not appeal to me.[116]

—Bertrand Russell

---

[115]Steven Weinberg, *The First Three Minutes* (New York: Basic Books, 1993), 154–55.
[116] Bertrand Russell, *Why I Am Not a Christian* (New York: Simon & Schuster, 1957), 32–33.

Wow. Steven Weinberg's view of the purpose of the universe and the meaning of life is a downer. The meaning of human life lies somewhere between farce and tragedy? Is that the most optimism and sense of purpose a Nobel Prize–winning physicist can muster? Bertrand Russell, also a Nobel Prize winner for literature, is just as morose. Both men were world-renowned atheists and, it seems, quite depressing.

An interesting phenomenon is that many modern atheists are rejecting the depressing **nihilism** of previous atheist generations. While they often say there is no real purpose of life or existence, they also say you can still have a purpose of your own making. This is sort of like saying you can have a purpose even though you don't really have one.

In summarizing the views of several prominent atheists on the subject of meaning and purpose, it seems they tend to have one of the following views:

1. *There is no purpose or meaning*—There is no purpose or meaning because the universe and human life are merely an accident. This seems to have been Steven Weinberg's and Bertrand Russell's view.
2. *There is biological purpose, but it's a puzzle as to why* —This was Jacques Monod's view.[117]
3. *Invent your own purpose and meaning*—This was Paul Kurtz's view. He stated that *"Life has no meaning per se,"* but we can create one for ourselves.[118]
4. *We can find and pursue purpose together*—This appears to be Peter Singer's view. Just find a purpose that seems to benefit everyone and pursue it.[119]

---

[117]Jacques Monod, *Chance and Necessity* (New York: Alfred A. Knopf, 1971), 21–22.
[118]Paul Kurtz, *Forbidden Fruit: The Ethics of Humanism* (Buffalo, NY: Prometheus Books, 1988), 240.
[119]Peter Singer, *How Are We to Live?: Ethics in an Age of Self-Interest* (Amherst, NY: Prometheus Books, 1995), 234–35.

For mankind to have a **shared universal purpose** for existence, it makes sense that a designer of mankind would be required. Otherwise, choose one of the four options above. If there is no designer, your choice is as good as anyone else's.

THEISTS AND ATHEISTS

PEOPLE WHO BELIEVE IN GOD LACK INTELLIGENCE

What is remarkable is the polar opposition between the religiosity of the American public at large and the atheism of the intellectual elite.[120]

—Richard Dawkins

It seems Richard Dawkins is befuddled by America's belief in God because it conflicts with the beliefs of those whom he calls *"the intellectual elite."* In other words, smart people are atheists, and people who are not smart believe in God.

Wait a minute. Since only 3.1 percent of Americans don't believe in God or a higher spiritual power and about 7 percent are agnostic, that implies about 90 percent of Americans are either ignorant, intellectually challenged, unenlightened or are otherwise delusional.[121]

---

[120]Richard Dawkins, *The God Delusion* (New York: Mariner Books, 2008), 127.
[121]*When Americans Say They Believe in God, What Do They Mean?*, Pew Research

That's essentially what Richard Dawkins asserts. He says people who believe in God are afflicted with a *"pernicious delusion."*[122] He also points to studies which suggest belief in God declines as education and IQ increase.

It seems America must be a scary place to live with so many intellectual dullards and deluded people. Yet even he has chosen to live here.

Just who are *"the intellectual elite"*? Are knowledge, truth and wisdom determined by people with a certain level of education or IQ? If so, what grade point average, college degree or IQ are needed to ascertain what is true and what is not? And, what if people with college educations and high IQs disagree? After all, smart people disagree all the time. Does a majority vote then determine truth? If so, who gets to vote?

What about people who have college degrees or who are college professors? Are they the intellectual elite who are overwhelmingly atheists? It seems not.

- *College educated*—It is true Americans with college degrees are more likely to call themselves atheists than non-college graduates—about 11 percent versus the national average of 3.1 percent. However, Americans with college degrees are just as likely to attend worship services each week as those without a degree and about 75 percent of college graduates are affiliated with a religion—about the same as non-college graduates.[123] So it doesn't really follow that people

Center, April 25, 2018, http://www.pewforum.org/2018/04/25/when-americans-say-they-believe-in-god-what-do-they-mean/

[122] Dawkins, *The God Delusion*, 52.

[123] "In America, Does More Education Equal Less Religion?", Pew Research Center, April 26, 2017, http://www.pewforum.org/2017/04/26/in-america-does-more-education-equal-less-religion/

who believe in God or who actively practice their religion lack intelligence.

- *College professors*—What about university professors? Do they believe in God? It seems they do. According to a 2009 survey in the *Sociology of Religion*, 55.8 percent of U.S. undergraduate professors believe in God and 19.2 percent believe in a "*higher power*." Another 13.1 percent don't know if there's a God. However, just 9.8 percent are atheists.[124]

If only about 10 percent of college graduates and college professors are atheists, one might start to wonder just exactly who Richard Dawkins considers to be the members of the atheist "*intellectual elite*." Are American college graduates and college professors not intelligent enough to be included? It seems they're not. Who then is in this tiny club?

It's also odd that Dawkins seems to limit the reputable, intelligent and scholarly to those with whom he agrees. For example, he states:

- "*Scholarly theologians*" view the Gospels as unreliable accounts of Jesus' life.
- "*Sophisticated*" Christians see the history in the Bible as inaccurate.
- Why "*sophisticated*" Christians stay in the church is a mystery.
- "*Reputable Bible scholars*" don't generally think the history in the Bible is reliable.[125]

---

[124]Neil Gross and Solon Simmons, "The Religiosity of American College and University Professors," *Sociology of Religion* (2009): 70:2, 113–114.
[125]Richard Dawkins, *The God Delusion*, 118, 120, 84, 122.

Given his own lack of background or training in history, theology or biblical studies, and his many incorrect statements about them, how is he qualified to dismiss the views of the many trained historians, archaeologists, theologians, and biblical scholars who disagree with his views?[126] And, what about the scientists who believe in God? What is Richard Dawkins to do with them?

It seems he simply dismisses them.

---

[126]For example, on page 58 of *The God Delusion*, Dawkins incorrectly states that Paul of Tarsus founded Christianity and Emperor Constantine made it the official religion of the Roman Empire. Christianity was actually founded by Jesus of Nazareth early in the first century. Paul of Tarsus, though important to Christianity, was one of Jesus' several apostles and wrote about a third of the text in the New Testament. Emperors Constantine and Licinius granted Christians the freedom to worship with the Edict of Milan in AD 313. However, it was Emperor Theodosius I (and his co-emperors) who effectively made Christianity the official religion of the Empire in AD 380 and AD 381.

REAL SCIENTISTS DON'T BELIEVE IN GOD

Richard Dawkins boldly asserts that elite scientists don't believe in God. And, while there are prominent examples of scientists who are theists, they are certainly in the minority and their very existence causes the bafflement of other scientists.[127] Is Dawkins correct? Does science require atheism of its legitimate practitioners?

Richard Dawkins points to the membership of the Royal Society, Britain's prestigious science academy, as proof that elite scientists don't believe in God. He proudly proclaims that 79 percent of the Fellows in the Society strongly disagree with the idea of a personal God.[128] Yet is this "proof" merely proof that atheism is a requirement to be in the club?

The British media reported that Dawkins and others in the Royal Society forced Michael Reiss to resign as the Society's director of science education in 2008. Reiss, a university science professor and part-time priest in the Church of England, had merely stated that creationism

---

[127]Dawkins, *The God Delusion*, 125.
[128]Ibid., 128.

should be acknowledged as a worldview.[129] He didn't even say he agreed with it. So, it seems merely acknowledging the existence of dissenting ideas can be dangerous in Dawkins' club.

Francis Collins, a scientist and Director of the U.S. National Institutes of Health, disagrees with Mr. Dawkins' assertion that belief in God is not scientific by turning the tables. He contends there is insufficient scientific evidence to support atheism. He maintains atheism is a belief system that exceeds the evidence to support it:

> *The major and inescapable flaw of Dawkins's claim that science demands atheism is that it goes beyond the evidence.*[130]

Back to the question, is it true that **real scientists** don't believe in God? Stephen Jay Gould, who was an atheist, evolutionary biologist, and Harvard and NYU professor, didn't think so. He made this observation about his fellow evolutionary biologists who believe in God:

> *Either half my colleagues are enormously stupid, or else the science of Darwinism is fully compatible with conventional religious beliefs—and equally compatible with atheism.*[131]

Probably enough said. It makes no sense to assert that real scientists don't believe in God. It's just not the case.

---

[129]http://www.bbc.co.uk/blogs/ni/2009/03/michael_reiss_why_i_resigned_f.html
[130]Francis Collins, *The Language of God* (New York: Free Press, 2007), 165.
[131]Ibid., 166.

ATHEISM IS
OBVIOUS

*The entirety of atheism is contained in this
response. Atheism is not a philosophy; it is
not even a view of the world; it is simply an
admission of the obvious.*[132]

—Sam Harris

This is quite a statement. Sam Harris asserts that atheism isn't a philosophy or a worldview; instead, it is a logical admission of the obvious. That's sort of like saying being a Republican or a Democrat isn't a philosophy or a worldview—being one or the other is just the logical acceptance of the obvious.

However, it's clear that people look at the same facts and reach different conclusions all the time. And, if atheism is so obvious, why do only 3.1 percent of Americans accept it as true? Perhaps it isn't so obvious.

---

[132]Sam Harris, *Letter to a Christian Nation* (New York: Alfred A. Knopf, 2006), 57.

That atheism isn't obvious is supported by Stephen Hawking and Richard Dawkins. Both felt the need to explain that, while on face value, the many fine-tuned laws of the universe and all of the species on Earth appear as though they were designed, they're not. They both readily acknowledge that life and the universe do look as though they were designed.

That's the most **obvious** conclusion. So, again, even to other prominent atheists, a universe without a designer isn't "*an admission of the obvious.*"

Sam Harris' statement just doesn't make sense.

ATHEISTS DON'T DO EVIL TO ADVANCE ATHEISM

Individual atheists may do evil things but they don't do evil things in the name of atheism.[133]

—Richard Dawkins

Atheists are people. They aren't perfect—no one is. Yet to say atheists don't do evil things in the name of atheism, as Richard Dawkins contends, seems odd indeed. It seems to be an idyllic view of atheism rather than reality.

Recent history bears out that atheists are indeed capable of doing evil in the name of the atheist cause. In November 2017, an angry militant atheist dressed in combat gear burst into a Texas church during the worship service. He killed twenty-six people and wounded twenty more.[134] Are all atheists like this? Thankfully, no. However, Mr.

---

[133]Dawkins, *The God Delusion*, 315.

[134]Max Jaeger, "Texas church shooter was a militant atheist," *NY Post*, November 6, 2017, https://nypost.com/2017/11/06/ex-friends-say-shooter-was-creepy-atheist-who-berated-religious-people/.

Dawkins' premise that atheists *"don't do evil things in the name of atheism,"* isn't reality. This is true of individuals and it's also true of nations.

WHAT ABOUT ATHEIST NATIONS?

Overtly atheist nations are a relatively new phenomenon. The Marxist communist nations of the twentieth century held to **atheism as a fundamental policy.** Karl Marx maintained that religion provided an illusion of happiness but that the abolition of religion was necessary for real happiness.[135]

Communist nations embraced this as social policy. If religion actually does cause more wars than anything else, we could assume that these nations which rejected belief in God would be the most peaceful—right? But is that what we see?

Rather than being the most peaceful and moral nations on Earth, Marxist atheist nations have been among the most brutal.

- *Soviet Union (USSR)*—Joseph Stalin led the Soviet Union from the mid-1920s to 1953. Timothy Snyder, a Yale University history professor, conveys that Stalin was responsible for the **deliberate killing of about six million of his own people.** Many were killed because of their race, others were political enemies, and many were killed because of their economic status.[136] Stalin also advanced policies to eliminate reli-

---

[135]Karl Marx, *Critique of Hegel's Philosophy of Right*, ed. Joseph O'Malley (Oxford, England: Oxford University Press, 1970), 131.

[136]Timothy Snyder, "Hitler vs. Stalin: Who Killed More?", *New York Review of Books*, March 10, 2011, http://www.nybooks.com/articles/2011/03/10/hitler-vs-stalin-who-killed-more/.

gion. During the 1920s and 1930s, most of the Russian Orthodox priests in the nation were shot or sent to prison camps.[137] He also invaded Finland and was complicit with Hitler as the Nazis invaded Poland. Stalin's atheism obviously didn't result in him being a nice guy.

- *People's Republic of China*—The second major atheist nation of the twentieth century was the People's Republic of China. Mao Zedong ruled the nation for ten years and presided over the communist party for four decades. Historian Frank Dikötter states that during Mao's *"great leap forward"* from 1958 to 1962 he was responsible for **the deaths of about forty-five million Chinese people.** Up to three million of them were executed or tortured to death. Millions more were knowingly starved.[138] Oh, and yes, Mao was a Marxist atheist.

- *Cambodia*—Pol Pot, the Marxist leader of the Khmer Rouge banned religion and prayer, closed schools, killed intellectuals and imposed a peasant-style economy. Under his leadership, over a million Cambodian people were tortured, executed and starved.[139] About **25 percent of the nation's population died.**

- *Cuba*—The body-count of those who were the victims of Fidel Castro's regime is still being tallied. However, on one occasion, 166 civilians and soldiers were executed. Just before their executions, seven

---

[137]*Revelations from the Russian Archives, Anti-Religious Campaigns*, (Washington, DC: U.S. Library of Congress, 2010), https://www.loc.gov/exhibits/archives/anti.html.

[138]Frank Dikötter, "Mao's Great Leap to Famine," *New York Times*, December 15, 2010, http://www.nytimes.com/2010/12/16/opinion/16iht-eddikotter16.html.

[139]Seth Mydans, "Death of Pol Pot," *New York Times*, April 17, 1998, https://www.nytimes.com/1998/04/17/world/death-pol-pot-pol-pot-brutal-dictator-who-forced-cambodians-killing-fields-dies.html.

pints of blood were extracted from each person and sold to Vietnam for $50 per pint.[140] The three and a half pints of blood they had left was just enough to keep them alive until their executions. Yes, Fidel Castro was a Marxist atheist who closed the churches in Cuba, took their property, and deported priests. He did evil to advance atheism.

Using just these four examples of recent Marxist atheist nations, it's obvious atheists have committed horrible evils to advance atheism. Richard Dawkins' assertion that they haven't is terribly inaccurate.

---

[140]Mary Anastasia O'Grady, "Counting Castro's Victims," *Wall Street Journal*, December 30, 2005, https://www.wsj.com/articles/SB113590852154334404

ATHEISTS RELY ON REASON, NOT FAITH

Atheism is nothing more than the noises rea-
sonable people make in the presence of unjus-
tified religious beliefs.
    It is time that we admitted that faith is
nothing more than the license religious people
give one another to believe when all reason
fails.[141]

—Sam Harris

When atheists say they rely on reason, and people who
believe in God rely on faith, this is generally what is
being implied—atheists **only** rely upon evidence and reason
in concluding there is no God, and theists and deists **only**
rely upon faith (not evidence and reason) in concluding
there is a God. However, are these broad assertions actually true? Are atheists purely rational and people who
believe in God not?

---

[141]Sam Harris, *Letter to a Christian Nation* (New York: Vintage Books, 2008), 51, 67.

105

DO ATHEISTS RELY ONLY ON EVIDENCE AND REASON?

Why are people atheists? To suggest all atheists have reached the conclusion there is no God based only upon deep analysis of evidence, is hardly true. Atheists choose to not believe in God for lots of reasons. For some, atheism was the belief-system they were taught as children. As an example, George Klein, a Swedish scientist and atheist, stated:

> *I am indeed an atheist. My attitude is not based on science but rather on faith, just as you have your faith. The absence of a creator, the nonexistence of God is my childhood faith, my adult belief, unshakable and holy.*[142]

For others, it was tragedy or disappointment—the death of a loved one, unanswered prayer, the bad example of someone professing belief in God, excessively rigid religious institutions or bad theology that caused them to embrace atheism. Atheism is not always just based on evidence and reason; emotion can also be involved. Were it not, why have atheists like Christopher Hitchens and Richard Dawkins been so angry?

Atheists do have a valid point that some theists and deists have accepted their views about God from those around them, rather than by evaluating the God-proposition themselves. And some have embraced the idea that God exists just because they want it to be true. However, don't atheists do the same thing?

---

[142]George Klein, *The Atheist and the Holy City* (Cambridge, MA: The MIT Press, 1990), 203.

. . . it is just as irrational to be influenced in one's beliefs by the hope that God does not exist as by the hope that God does exist.[143]

—*Thomas Nagel*

It's true that not everything we believe is based on hard evidence. As children, we tended to accept the things our parents told us as being true. We believed them because we respected and trusted them. We did the same with our school teachers.

As adults, we still accept things from those we trust. We all do this because we don't have the time or tools to personally evaluate the truth of everything we're told. This is true of those who believe in God and those who don't.

WHAT IS FAITH?

When people say they have faith in God, they generally mean three things. First, they **believe** God exists. Second, they **rely** on or trust in God's existence. Third, they **seek** to know and follow God. However, faith isn't based merely upon blind wishful thinking. It's generally based upon evidence—personal experience, historical accounts of God's interactions with people, morality and natural theology (how the universe works). It's also based on reason.

IS FAITH BLIND OR DEVOID OF REASON?

What of the notion attributed to Soren Kierkegaard, the Danish philosopher, that belief in God is a blind leap of faith? The first problem is he never actually said faith is a

---

[143]Thomas Nagel, *The Last Word* (New York: Oxford University Press, 1997), 131.

blind leap. The leap or jump he was talking about was from mankind's state of innocence to sinfulness.

The solution to the state of sinfulness was forgiveness—through faith in Christ.[144] And, Kierkegaard wasn't saying the faith decision was to be made based on no information or thinking. After all, he was a philosopher, thinking is what he did!

However, the faith decision was made with the knowledge that reason alone couldn't provide all of the answers about God. To him, faith was a passionate **response** to God that *"begins precisely where thinking leaves off."*[145] The second problem is Kierkegaard's religion, Christianity, doesn't teach that belief in God should be based on blind faith—it's to be based on evidence, reasoning and revelation (insight) from God.[146]

Richard Dawkins has claimed that belief in God is *"blind trust"* in spite of evidence to the contrary. His implication seems to be that any belief in God is inherently opposed to reason. Francis Collins disagrees and responded to Dawkins' claim with a simple observation:

> *Dawkins's definition of faith is "blind trust, in the absence of evidence, even in the teeth of evidence." That certainly does not describe the faith of most serious believers throughout history, nor of most of those in my personal acquaintance.*[147]

---

[144]Søren Kierkegaard, *The Concept of Anxiety* (New York: Liveright Publishing Corp., 2014), 36–42, 46–50, 67, 140–41.

[145]Søren Kierkegaard, *Fear and Anxiety* (Princeton, NJ: Princeton University Press, 1954), 64, 77, 131.

[146]Psalm 19:1–4; Matthew 1:22–23; 3:1–6; 8:14–17; 13:34–35; 21:1–5; 27:3–10; John 2:18–21; 14:8–11; Acts 2:22–28; 17:2–4, 16–17, 29–31; 9:1–22; 18:1–4, 18–19; Romans 1:18–20

[147]Collins, *The Language of God*, 164.

When atheists imply that all people who believe in God do so without assessing available evidence and without the use of reason, it's simply not true. Even theists possess brains and they too tend to use them.

KNOWLEDGE, SELF AND FREE WILL

SCIENCE IS THE ONLY SOURCE OF RATIONAL KNOWLEDGE

Science is the only philosophical construct we have to determine truth with any degree of reliability.[148]

—Harold Kroto

There is an old saying, "If the only tool you have is a hammer, then everything looks like a nail." The point of this saying is simple—our perspective and solutions are impaired by the limits of our tool kit.

It seems some scientists have been afflicted by this problem. In some cases, the only tool kit they acknowledge is a scientific one. Harold Kroto, a Nobel Prize winner for chemistry, seems to have been one who suffered from this affliction. To him, science was the only way to reliably determine truth. Yet is this really the case?

---

[148]https://www.theguardian.com/commentisfree/andrewbrown/2011/jul/04/harry-kroto-science-truth

SCIENTIFIC TOOLS

There are some things that science is really good at. Scientific disciplines are really useful in exploring and understanding physical things like planets, rocks, chemicals and energy. They're also really good at exploring and understanding living things like plants, animals, people and bacteria.

However, scientific disciplines aren't the only disciplines whereby we can rationally develop knowledge and establish truths. There are other tools in the tool kit—philosophy, language, mathematics[149] and history are just a few. The notion that rational knowledge is only ascertainable by science is to say your favorite tool is the **only tool**. That's just not true. In fact, if it weren't for philosophy, language and mathematics, science wouldn't be very scientific.

WHAT ABOUT HISTORY?

We know a lot about George Washington. We know he was the commanding general of the colonial armies, he was married to Martha, where he lived, what he did, when he died, the significance of his life and the legacy of freedom he left that is now the United States of America. We don't know this through science. We know it through history—and we know it reliably. Thousands of written documents and historical artifacts tell us about him and what he did.

---

[149]There is debate in academic circles as to whether mathematics is a science or a separate discipline that provides the tools for science to test and measure physical things. However, it's clear, without mathematical tools, science would not have emerged from the discipline of philosophy.

WHAT ABOUT SOCIAL SCIENCES?

There has been a trend to call academic disciplines "science" that have little resemblance to the natural sciences. Sociology, political science, anthropology, economics, demography and psychology are examples. While all of these disciplines utilize similar tools as the natural sciences, they are not science in the same sense. However, they do convey reliable truth. Here's an example.

Economics is a great discipline. It's what I majored in as an undergraduate student. Like the natural sciences, it uses philosophy, language and mathematics as tools with which to build. It also acknowledges individual and group psychology. It shares some of the same attributes as the natural sciences in that both can be descriptive, predictive and quantitative.

However, economics isn't one of the natural sciences. And, though it isn't, we still reliably discern truth through it. It tells us about unemployment, inflation, wage rates, the money supply, interest rates and economic cycles. We rely on this information to make decisions every day. But, though it's empirical, it's not really "science."

SCIENTISM

Ian Hutchinson, a nuclear science professor at MIT, calls statements like Mr. Kroto's "scientism." He defines scientism as follows:

> *Scientism is the belief that all valid knowledge is science. Scientism says, or at least implicitly assumes, that rational knowledge is scientific, and everything else that claims the status of*

knowledge is just superstition, irrationality, emotion, or nonsense.[150]

Hutchinson, a scientist, disagrees with the notion that rational knowledge can only be known through the discipline of science. He readily acknowledges other disciplines are valuable too.

Francis Collins, one of the world's leading genetic scientists, observes, when it comes to learning about God, the tools of science aren't necessarily even the right ones to use:

> *If God exists, then He must be outside of the natural world, and therefore the tools of science are not the right ones to learn about Him.*[151]

Harold Kroto isn't the only scientist who demonstrates scientism's tendencies. Stephen Hawking famously stated *"philosophy is dead,"* though most philosophy professors would likely not agree.[152]

The narrow view that the tools of your discipline, in this case science, are the only tools to use to establish knowledge and truth makes no sense. There are other tools in the tool kit and times when they—not science—are the best ones to use.

[150]Ian Hutchinson, *Monopolizing Knowledge* (Belmont, MA: Fias Publishing, 2011), 2.
[151]Francis Collins, *The Language of God* (New York: Free Press, 2007), 30.
[152]Stephen Hawking, *The Grand Design* (New York: Bantam Books, 2012), 5.

YOU'VE GOT
NO SOUL

*Science provides clear-cut answers to all of
the questions on the list: there is no free will,
there is no mind distinct from the brain, there
is no soul, no self, no person that supposedly
inhabits your body, that endures over its lifes-
pan, and that might even out last it. So, introspection must be wrong.*[153]

—Alex Rosenberg

Why is whether we have a **self** or a **soul** important to atheists? Apart from curiosity, why would these terms matter? It seems that to some, the idea that we have **being** apart from matter or a soul that matter alone didn't create is a problem. If we have a soul apart from matter or that didn't emerge from matter, it opens the door for the

---

[153]Alex Rosenberg, *The Atheists Guide to Reality* (New York: W.W. Norton, 2011), 147.

possibility of the existence of the nonphysical and the existence of God. That's a door many don't want to open. The first big challenge with the idea we don't have a soul, as Alex Rosenberg points out, is that our own minds tell us we do. Our thoughts tell us that we have individual identity, unique ideas and perspectives, self-awareness, introspection, intent, self-direction, the ability to control our bodies and the ability to affect the things around us. Our thoughts tell us our "self" is in charge. But, because this disagrees with what Rosenberg says science tells us, he claims our *"introspection must be wrong"*—what our thoughts tell us about ourselves can't be trusted.

This is some concept. If what Rosenberg says is true, how could you trust your own thoughts about anything? Now that would be a problem. Also, the examples Rosenberg gives to support his claim have primarily to do with perception rather than introspection.[154]

Yet we know that a straw only appears to bend when inserted into a glass of water. Our conscious thoughts are logical enough to figure this out and they can be trusted.

WHAT IS CONSCIOUSNESS?

You can't really have a conversation about "self" or "soul" without talking about consciousness, but that makes for a difficult conversation. It's difficult for two reasons. The first is that consciousness and your brain go together and, as Susan Blakemore points out, the brain is reportedly *"the most complex object in the known universe."*[155] The second reason is that it seems no one—not physicists, psycholo-

---

[154] Ibid., 146–63.
[155] Susan Blakemore, *Consciousness: A Very Short Introduction* (Oxford, England: Oxford University Press, 2017), 17.

gists, philosophers, biologists or neuroscientists—understands the nature of consciousness or how it came to be. They do have some ideas, which can be summarized without too much difficulty, but the fact that no one really knows is telling.

Let's start by looking at what consciousness is not. It's not non-consciousness. It's also not unconsciousness, though the two do work together. But it does include dreams and semi-consciousness. As you can tell, it gets complicated quickly.

When people talk about consciousness, they generally include: sensation, perception, external-awareness, reaction, thought, memory, self-awareness, emotion, intuition, values, reasoning, dreams, imagination, conclusions, intent, initiation (will), introspection, perspective, and identity.

All these things are extraordinary. Yet the most extraordinary are the things totally unique to you. It's your sense of **I**, **me** and **my** but it's also your unique perspective, thoughts, emotions, plans, desires, opinions and ideas. This is your unique self.

THE SOURCE OF SELF?

There are a lot of hypotheses related to "self." Please be patient as we cover just five of them at a very high level. This won't take long. A key idea to keep in mind as we review them is how different they are. Let's start with an idea that became popular in the 1900s.

1. *Materialism*—Materialism states that your consciousness is purely a material phenomenon. You do have consciousness and thought, but your sense of self, being a person, or of even having a first-person point-of-view is an illusion of your introspection. If this is

true, we should probably take the words I, me and my out of the dictionary. Colin McGinn made a blunt assessment of this view:

Materialism says there is nothing more to the mind than the brain as currently conceived. The mind is made of meat. It is meat, neither more nor less. . . . We might as well call materialism "meatism."[156]

2. **Natural Mysterianism**—Rather than materialism, McGinn holds to what he calls natural mysterianism. This is the view that people have consciousness, which has the physical brain as its "seat" and is naturally supported by the brain. However, it's unexplainable by the physical brain; it's a mystery.[157] He rejects God as being its source, but is unaware of any natural force which *"might explain how ever-expanding lumps of matter might have developed an inner conscious life."*[158] He says:

It looks as if with consciousness a new kind of reality has been injected into the universe, instead of just a recombination of the old realities.[159]

McGinn states that neither physics nor natural selection provide an answer for how consciousness began.[160] He thinks it happened naturally but that we'll never figure out how. He also acknowledges the existence of

[156]Colin McGinn, *The Mysterious Flame* (New York: Basic Books, 1999), 18.
[157]Ibid., 4–5, 28–29.
[158]Ibid., 15.
[159]Ibid., 13.
[160]Ibid., 81–82.

self and our subjective awareness but doesn't know how they came to be either.[161]

3. *Naturalistic Dualism*—David Chalmers proposes the bold possibility that consciousness may be a basic building block of nature. This would liken it to space, time and matter. It would also mean it was universally present at the beginning of the universe. Though it's difficult to imagine how this would work, he advances the idea that consciousness is a result of "*basic laws of nature.*"[162] He calls this idea **naturalistic dualism.**[163] However, he doesn't really present a view as to how our sense of self could have emerged.

4. *Panpsychism*—Thomas Nagel sees problems with these other approaches. He doesn't see how consciousness, which is subjective even at the lowest levels, could have emerged from nonconscious matter. Therefore, he proposes an even more daring alternative for consideration—what if consciousness is inherent in matter? What if all matter is somehow imbued with consciousness? This is called **panpsychism**—everything has consciousness.

5. *Dualism*—Other than those proposed by McGinn and Chalmers, there are many flavors of dualism. They're generally the idea that consciousness (or the soul) and the brain are different—consciousness is somehow nonphysical and the brain is physical.

These are just five of the many ideas being explored and tested. There are lots more. However, if consciousness with a sense of self and being exists (and right now my self is

---

[161]Ibid., 162–65.

[162]David Chalmers, *The Conscious Mind: In Search of a Fundamental Theory* (New York: Oxford University Press, 1996), 128.

[163]He states that naturalistic dualism is a dualism of "properties" rather than "substances"— it's one substance with two properties.

telling me it does), there are really only three options as to how it originated:

1. *It developed.* If consciousness developed, it either did so with help or without it. If it developed **with help**, it seems an intelligent conscious cause would be required. If it developed **without help**, it would require a law of nature or a known process in nature for it to do so. However, there is no known natural process that can develop consciousness, and many scientists and philosophers readily concede that natural selection couldn't have done it.[164] If an unknown law of nature is its source, the law would likely have been present at the big bang.

2. *It is inherent.* If consciousness is in everything, it was present in matter at the beginning of the universe. However, if the universe had a beginning that was nonphysical, consciousness' source would also be nonphysical. That source would also have to be intelligent because consciousness (as we know it) can't exist apart from information.

3. *It was given.* This view holds that consciousness, with its sense of a unique self that possesses unique perspective, introspection, creativity, reason, opinions and the ability to make decisions and initiate, exceeds the known laws of nature and exceeds the probability of development through nature. Therefore, its source was not solely natural.

In either of these three scenarios, it seems an intelligent conscious cause would be required. Whether consciousness

---

[164]McGinn, *The Mysterious Flame*, 81 and Thomas Nagel, *Mind & Cosmos, Why the Materialist Neo-Darwinian Conception of Nature Is Almost Certainly Wrong* (New York: Oxford University Press, 2012),11.

was developed, the result of a law of nature or inherent in nature, intelligence would be needed to precede it. Theists call this intelligent cause God.

It's interesting that Rosenberg, McGinn, Chalmers, and Nagel are all philosophers and self-described atheists. With the exception of Alex Rosenberg, they all say self exists. None of them can point to its source with any certainty, but all of them prefer to believe it's not God.

John Eccles is not a philosopher; he's a Nobel Prize–winning neuroscientist and knows a lot about the human brain. Like philosophers and his scientific colleagues, he has long pondered the questions of consciousness and self. Given the deficiency of purely naturalistic options, he has concluded that its source was beyond nature:

> *Since materialist solutions fail to account for our experienced uniqueness, I am constrained to attribute the uniqueness of the Self or Soul to a supernatural spiritual creation.*[165]

What can we conclude from all this? Well, the idea that you do have a self or a soul as a part of your consciousness, which resides in your brain, seems to be a generally accepted view. Consciousness' source, in turn, seems to require an intelligent cause. However, the idea that you don't have a self or a soul only makes sense if your own conscious thoughts can't really be trusted.

That would be a peculiar way to live.

---

[165] John C. Eccles, *Evolution of the Brain: Creation of the Soul* (New York: Routledge, 1989), 237.

YOU JUST THINK YOU HAVE FREE WILL

Above the level of the smallest numbers of fermions and bosons, the universe is almost totally deterministic. That means that everything we do is just the consequence of the laws of nature and events in the distant past.[166]

The fact that the mind is the brain guarantees there is no free will.[167]

—Alex Rosenberg

According to Alex Rosenberg's way of thinking, none of us have free will. The brain is a physical organ and is subject to the physical laws of nature and external events. These influences direct the neural connections in our brain to make decisions that appear to be our own free choices but, in reality, are not. Free will is just an illusion.

---

[166]Rosenberg, *The Atheists Guide to Reality*, 292.
[167]Rosenberg, *The Atheists Guide to Reality*, 195.

How could Rosenberg reasonably reach this conclusion? Like everyone else, he probably picks out his clothes to wear in the morning, chooses what to order at the local diner, selects what to watch on television, and decides when to go to bed. He likely made a decision to accept his teaching position at Duke University and probably decides what to include in his lesson plans. He probably makes dozens, if not hundreds, of decisions every day. How is it then that he believes he doesn't make these decisions freely?

Alex Rosenberg sees the universe through the eyes of scientism, which he claims is committed to **determinism**.[168] He sees physics, chemistry and biology as having no real design, plans or purposes—they just are. Since we are merely biological life-forms, we have no designs, plans or purposes either—we just are. We possess consciousness and the ability to think, but we're sort of like ants and beavers who do what they do because they're compelled to do it.[169] So, if our conscious minds tell us we make decisions, it's merely an illusion.[170] After all, as he says, scientism is *"committed to a purpose-free mind."*[171]

At its core, determinism is based on the notion that the universe is a closed system of cause and effect—sort of like a set of balls on a billiard table continuously bouncing into and off each other. That's a logical assumption based on the idea that everything has a physical cause. However, this idea has its limitations as we'll see in a minute.

According to Rosenberg's determinism, criminals aren't really at fault. Crime is like a disease; it's not a decision. Therefore, criminals aren't really guilty and don't deserve

---

[168]There are many forms of determinism. Rosenberg seems to advocate incompatible (or hard) determinism.
[169]Rosenberg, *The Atheists Guide to Reality*, 215–16.
[170]Ibid., 205.
[171]Ibid., 206.

punishment. (Though, to protect others, it may be necessary to incarcerate them.)[172] Likewise, those who possess wealth don't really deserve it because their wealth wasn't really the result of their plans and purposes.[173] I guess this means none of his students deserve a grade on their exams—they presumably don't have plans or purposes either.

Are our decisions really just the result of the laws of physics, chemical reactions, neurons firing in our heads and events in the distant past? Without neurons in our brains, we couldn't think, but is that what dictates our decisions? Does an architect really design a high-rise building only because (like a very large ant) she is compelled to do so? Why does one person dive into a freezing river to save a child while others watch in fear? Do physics, chemistry and biology not tell everyone to do the same thing?

Let's start by looking at **free will**. What is it? Well, it clearly doesn't mean your choices are unlimited. You can't choose to be seven feet tall if you're not, or choose to buy a Ferrari if you have no money. There are things you can't, in reality, choose. Your choices are also not free from physics, chemistry and biology. If your taste buds tell your brain cauliflower tastes terrible, you likely won't be able to convince it otherwise.

And, your choices aren't free from external influences. When a police officer tells you to pull over, you generally do it. So, it seems clear that your choices are not unlimited nor are they free from other influences. Yet are your choices really yours?

Though we're limited in our choices and externally influenced, our choices are still genuine. We initiate things,

---

[172]Ibid., 293–95.
[173]Ibid., 220.

change our minds, make plans, create works of art and go out of our way to help others because we want to—not just because we have to or are influenced to do so. So, it seems what we think we do and what determinism says we do are in conflict.

DETERMINISM'S CHALLENGES

We do see cause and effect in nature. However, the question is whether we **only** see cause and effect and whether we see it throughout nature. Does determinism really make sense? It makes sense if you're willing to overlook the obvious.

- *It contradicts perception*—Determinism contradicts what our own consciousness tells us about reality. We **think** we are making choices and plans and **think** we have our own reasons for doing the things we do. If our own consciousness can't be trusted in regard to our most basic perceptions of reality and our sense of self, then our thoughts can't be trusted about anything—including our thoughts about determinism.[174]

Rupert Sheldrake, a biochemist, points out, "*If materialism is true, all bodies, including yours and mine, are essentially unconscious.*"[175] He makes a good point, if we don't really make decisions of our own volition, we might as well be unconscious. (Zombies come to mind.)

---

[174]Philosophers who hold to determinism state that your decisions, while real, are actually dictated by purely natural phenomenon. Therefore, your decisions are epiphenomenon—subsets of the actual causes.

[175]Rupert Sheldrake, *The Science Delusion: Freeing the Spirit of Enquiry* (London, England: Hodder & Stoughton Ltd., 2013), 127.

- *It's not universal*—Another problem with determinism is that it doesn't seem to operate throughout nature. The sub-atomic level seems to be free of determinism. As Mr. Sheldrake states, *"with the recognition of the uncertainty principle in quantum physics, it became clear that indeterminism was an essential feature of the physical world."*[176] That results in the question, if indeterminism is a feature of quantum physics, why can it not also be a feature elsewhere in nature?

- *The universe may not be closed*—If the universe had a beginning from a nonphysical source, which it did, then the universe isn't a closed system. At minimum, on day one, it wasn't closed. The universe is also continually expanding—into nothing. (That's sort of weird.) And, scientists now believe the amount of dark energy in the universe is increasing![177] Dark energy is sort of an energy field filling empty space.[178] Astrophysicist Sarah Salviander estimates that, as the universe expands, the equivalent of about five billion-trillion-trillion-trillion nuclear power plants' worth of energy is being added to the universe every second![179] How is this possible in a closed universe?

---

[176]Ibid., 18. As a side note, Heisenberg's *Principle of Indeterminacy* states that the location of a particle and its velocity cannot be simultaneously estimated in space-time. Causation cannot be detected.

[177]Ethan Siegel, "Dark Energy May Not Be a Constant, Which Would Lead to a Revolution in Physics," *Forbes*, January 31, 2019, https://www.forbes.com/sites/startswithabang/2019/01/31/dark-energy-may-not-be-a-constant-which-would-lead-to-a-revolution-in-physics/#52266b3ab737.

[178]Dark energy is thought to comprise about 68 percent of the universe. As the universe expands, new dark energy fills the new space and the density of dark energy throughout the universe remains constant. However, surprising new research shows what was thought to be a constant density of dark energy throughout space may actually be increasing.

[179]Sarah Salviander, *God, the expanding universe, and dark energy*, January 23, 2019, https://sixdayscience.com/.

Yet, even if the universe is closed now, there is no compelling reason to believe we are not genuine sources of causation—we can **choose** to make things happen that otherwise would not have. We are not the billiard balls. We are the ones who play billiards.

Of course there is cause and effect in the universe and in our daily lives. The laws of nature, our genetic traits, our environment, our families and external events do influence us. However, they don't totally dictate what we do. Max Planck, a father of modern physics, acknowledged determinism's influence on our lives, but he also saw its limit.[180]

> *I might put the matter in another way and say that the freedom of the ego here and now, and its independence of the causal chain, is a truth that comes from the immediate dictate of the human consciousness.*
>
> *Our consciousness, which after all is the most immediate source of cognition, assures us that free will is supreme.*[181]

Why does any of this matter? It matters because, if determinism is true, you are essentially a puppet of nature not really responsible for what you do, or worse than that— you're a thing.

Your introspection tells you that you are a person, a human **being** with a unique **self** who really makes decisions, loves, dreams, remembers, plans, builds, values, creates and can **cause** change in the world around you. And, if you and I are unique beings who have at least some limited mastery over nature, perhaps there could be one more unique being out there with mastery over nature—God.

[180] Max Planck, *Where Is Science Going?* (New York: W.W. Norton, 1932), 165.
[181] Max Planck, *The Philosophy of Physics* (New York: W.W. Norton, 1936), 32–33.

RELIGION

RELIGION RUINS EVERYTHING

*. . . people of faith are in their different ways
planning your and my destruction, and the
destruction of all hard-won human attain-
ments that I have touched upon. Religion poisons everything.*[182]

—Christopher Hitchens

Christopher Hitchens saw religion as a great evil that
ruins and poisons everything it touches. He saw people
who possess religious faith as destructive to humanity and
human progress. And, his assertion that religion ruins
everything wasn't just limited to selected religions or specific religious institutions, it included everyone who practices any religion—animism, pantheism, monotheism or
polytheism. Is he correct?

---

[182] Christopher Hitchens, *God Is Not Great* (New York: Hachette Book Group,
2007), 13.

At first it seems difficult to test Hitchens' assertion. It seems difficult because most people on Earth actually do have some religious beliefs they formally or informally practice. So, saying religion or religious people ruin everything is sort of like saying people who breathe air ruin everything.

If most people have religious beliefs, how can you be sure the problem is their religious ideals and not something else? Maybe the problem isn't their religion, maybe it's human pride, greed, selfishness, fear, rage or another flaw most of us seem to share.

Christopher Hitchens diagnosed himself and the human race as possessing the flaws of stupidity and selfishness. If he's correct, then perhaps we are the real problem, rather than religion.

> *Given this overwhelming tendency to stupidity and selfishness in myself and among our species, it is somewhat surprising to find the light of reason penetrating at all.*[183]

That religious people and religious institutions have done harmful things is clear. Hitchens is right about that. It's also clear that some religion's teachings seem morally superior to others. However, religious people and institutions have also done amazing things to help people. And, in addition to worshiping God, a general theme in most religions is the advancement of morality. Religion generally seeks to curb evil behavior rather than condone it.

Upon reflection, it is possible to test whether Hitchens' claim that religion ruins everything might be correct. Instead of looking at individual people, what about

---

[183] Ibid., 77.

nations? If he's correct, nations with the most people who do not believe in God should be more moral, enjoy greater human progress and be more fulfilled than those who do. While not perfect, this sounds like a reasonable test. However, as we have already seen, the world's atheist nations have consistently been among the most brutal and oppressive on Earth. So it seems Hitchens' claim falls short.

RELIGION IS THE BIGGEST CAUSE OF WAR

More wars have been fought in the name of religion than anything else.

—Anonymous (paraphrased)

A glance at history, or at the pages of any newspaper, reveals that ideas which divide one group of human beings from another, only to unite them in slaughter, generally have their roots in religion.[184]

—Sam Harris

The number of atheists who claim religion is the greatest cause of war throughout history is astounding. You can see the claim on atheist websites and in a variety of books. It's one of those claims repeated so frequently that few people take the time to actually challenge it. However, it's really

---

[184]Sam Harris, *The End of Faith* (New York: W.W. Norton & Company, 2005), 12.

137

not that difficult to test. And, after you do test it, the notion that more wars are caused by religion than anything else is a bit odd because it's simply not even close to being true.

Let's start by taking a look at America.

WHAT ABOUT THE UNITED STATES?

The United States is one of the most religious nations on earth. Over 90 percent of Americans believe in God. If religion **causes** war, it would therefore follow that America's domestic conflicts and foreign wars have primarily been caused by religion or America's desire to force its religious beliefs upon others. But is this what our daily lives and history actually show?

1. *Crime*—Day-to-day crime and conflict in America seems to have almost nothing to do with religious beliefs. It's interesting, there were 1,163,146 violent crimes in the United States in 2013. Yet, only 1,223 crimes were reported to have been motivated by a religious bias.[185] And, while that's still too many, it's only 1/10th of 1 percent of violent crime. If religion really **caused** conflict, you would think more violence would actually be attributed to it. But, in almost none of the crimes in the U.S. do the headlines read "Baptist violence escalates!" It's also interesting that we don't see prison gangs of Catholics, Presbyterians or Jews killing each other. That's because America's belief in God isn't really the cause of our internal conflicts.

2. *American Wars*—What about America's wars? Does America's belief in God cause our wars? Let's take a

---

[185]*2013 Hate Crime Statistics* (Washington, DC: U.S. Department of Justice, 2013), https://ucr.fbi.gov/hate-crime/2013/topic-pages/victims/victims_final.

look. Depending on whether you just count officially declared wars or all military conflicts, the United States has engaged in about twelve wars since its birth. There was the Revolutionary War to break free from England, the War of 1812 (again versus England), the Indian Wars, the Mexican War, the Civil War, the Spanish-American War, World War I, World War II, the Korean Conflict, the Vietnam War, the Gulf War, and the War on Terror. Of all these wars, only the War on Terror was caused by religion. And it wasn't fought by the United States to advance its religious beliefs; it was fought to defend America and its allies against religious extremists who attacked us.

In all, since our nation's birth, about 970,000 U.S. soldiers have died in the theater of war. America's bloodiest war ever was the U.S. Civil War—about 530,000 Union and Confederate soldiers died.[186] The war was mostly about slavery, states' rights and economics. It wasn't about religion. In the one war about religion, the War on Terror, about 6,915 have died.[187] That's about 7/10ths of 1 percent of all U.S. soldiers killed in war.

So, using the United States as an example, it doesn't look like belief in God and religion is inherently the cause of crime or war. It's not. And, of all the wars fought, religion was the cause of only one.

---

[186]*America's Wars* (Washington, DC: U.S. Dept. of Veterans Affairs, 2017). https://www.va.gov/opa/publications/factsheets/fs_americas_wars.pdf.
[187]Kurtis Lee, "Memorial Day: The number of Americans who have died in battle since the Revolutionary War," *Los Angeles Times*, May 29, 2017, http://www.latimes.com/nation/la-na-memorial-day-20170529-htmlstory.html.

WHAT ABOUT THE GREAT ANCIENT EMPIRES?

Did major ancient empires fight their wars to advance religious beliefs or were their gods merely called upon for assistance to secure their own desires? Let's look at one of the biggest—the Roman Empire.

After reviewing histories written by the ancient Roman historians—Appian, Eutropius and Tacitus,—it's clear that Roman wars and civil wars were generally motivated by a desire for land, resources, wealth, power or self-defense.[188] Of the many foreign wars and civil wars Rome fought from its founding in the eighth century BC through the first century AD, none were attributed by these historians to religion.[189] Even the Jewish revolt of AD 66 wasn't about religion; it was the result of the oppressive policies of the Roman procurator.[190]

So, during the roughly 900 years covered by these historians collectively, no wars seem to have been started to advance religion. However, during this time, Rome was engaged in almost continuous war as it conquered peoples and kingdoms that compose most of what is now modern Europe, northern Africa, the Middle East and Asia Minor. They became one of the largest, richest and most powerful empires in the world. Yet religion wasn't the motivation for the expansion of their empire or their wars.

---

[188] Appian's *Foreign Wars*, Eutropius' *Abridgement of Roman History* and Tacitus' *Histories*.

[189] The Romans generally allowed conquered nations to freely exercise their religions. However, from the first century through the early fourth century, various Imperial edicts were imposed that sought to eliminate Judaism and Christianity within the Empire. Because of this, the Jews revolted again in AD 135. The Christians did not rebel.

[190] Tacitus, *The Histories* (London: Penguin Classics, 2009), 250. Also, first-century Jewish historian, Josephus, records in *Wars of the Jews*, that the revolt was caused by Florus, the procurator, and his heavy-handed approach (2.14–2.17).

HAVEN'T THERE BEEN WARS TO ADVANCE RELIGION?

It's obvious there have been wars fought to advance religious beliefs and to suppress those who held to non-conforming beliefs. This happened during the Crusades and the Thirty Years War in Europe. There has also been persecution of those who held to conflicting religious beliefs. The Spanish Inquisition during the fifteenth century is a great example. However, in the grand span of history, these seem to be exceptions to the rule.

WHAT DO THE NUMBERS SHOW?

Okay, let's cut to the chase. What do the numbers throughout history really show? Have more wars been fought in the name of religion and caused more deaths than anything else? Not according to the *Encyclopedia of Wars*. Based on an analysis of the data presented, it appears that of all known historical conflicts, 7 percent were caused primarily by religion. These wars accounted for just 2 percent of all known deaths from warfare.[191] That's hardly consistent with the claims made by many atheists.

Nigel Barber, a biopsychologist and atheist, agrees with the conclusions of the *Encyclopedia of Wars*:

> *Religion is rarely the intrinsic cause of conflict and explicitly religious wars, such as the medieval Crusades are rare.*[192]

[191] Alan Lurie, Is Religion the Cause of Most Wars?, *Huffington Post*, June 10, 2012, https://www.huffingtonpost.com/rabbi-alan-lurie/is-religion-the-cause-of-_b_1400766.html.

[192] Nigel Barber, "Is Religion Better at Making Peace or Making War?", *Psychology Today*, August 1, 2012, https://www.psychologytoday.com/us/blog/the-human-beast/201208/is-religion-better-making-peace-or-making-war.

Yes, there have been wars motivated by religion, but to say that religion or belief in God is the primary cause of the world's conflicts is grossly inaccurate. It makes no sense for atheists to keep saying this when it's absolutely not what history shows.

MYSTICISM IS RATIONAL BUT RELIGION IS NOT

Mysticism is a rational enterprise. Religion is not. The mystic has recognized something about the nature of consciousness prior to thought, and this recognition is susceptible to rational discussion. The mystic has reasons for what he believes, and these reasons are empirical.[193]
The roiling mystery of the world can be analyzed with concepts (this is science), or it can be experienced free of concepts (this is mysticism).[194]

—Sam Harris

Sam Harris contends mysticism is rational but religion is not. This would likely sound strange to most Americans—especially when he states that mysticism is *"experienced free of concepts."* (How is something experienced free of

---

[193]Sam Harris, *The End of Faith* (New York: W.W. Horton & Co., 2005), 221.
[194]Ibid.

concepts rational?) Most Americans would probably see mysticism as either religion without God or as some form of meditation-based pursuit. They would likely equate it to a form of religious practice. So, what does Harris mean by *mysticism*?

WHAT IS MYSTICISM?

Let's start by looking at the generally understood meaning of mysticism. Merriam-Webster provides several definitions. Here are the first two:[195]

1. the experience of mystical union or direct communion with ultimate reality reported by mystics
2. the belief that direct knowledge of God, spiritual truth, or ultimate reality can be attained through subjective experience (such as intuition or insight)

Given the context of his statements and the common meanings of the word, it seems Sam Harris' mysticism is the experience of some sort of mystical union with ultimate reality.

IS SAM HARRIS' MYSTICISM RELIGION?

Harris points to Buddha, Shankara, Padmasambhava, Nagarjuna, and Longchenpa as great mystic heroes.[196] However, just randomly picking two of these mystics shows that they were actually very religious.

---

[195] https://www.merriam-webster.com/, Other definitions include: 3) vague speculation : a belief without sound basis, 4) a theory postulating the possibility of direct and intuitive acquisition of ineffable knowledge or power

[196] Harris, *The End of Faith*, 215.

- *Shankara* —Shankara was a Hindu philosopher who lived in the eighth or ninth century. His teachings became the Advaita Vedanta school of Hindu philosophy and included the worship of Hindu gods.

Shankara did recognize the important role worship and devotion play in the early stages of the aspirant's way to self-realization. He wrote many hymns in praise of the popular deities like Siva, Vishnu, and the Divine Mother to help ordinary people move towards their ultimate realization.[197]

—Vensus George

The recognition and worship of deities was an important part of Shankara's theology in that it was supposed to help move adherents along the path, first to God (*Saguna Brahman*), and then to unity with ultimate true reality (*Nirguna Brahman*). Meditation was also key in removing ignorance and moving a person toward absolute consciousness. The objective was to realize that your eternal ultimate self (*Atman*) is the same thing as formless and incomprehensible ultimate reality (*Nirguna Brahman*).[198]

Worshiping deities and meditation rituals as a means of achieving unity with Ultimate Reality sounds a lot like religion—probably because it is religion. It's just religion without a single God as the Ultimate Reality. In this system, the gods are a part of Ultimate Reality and so are you. The unity of your own eternal self with "indescribable" Ultimate Reality is the goal.

---

[197]Vensus George, *Authentic Human Destiny, The Paths of Shankara and Heidegger* (Washington, DC: The Council for Research in Values and Philosophy, 1998), 355.
[198]http://www.newworldencyclopedia.org/entry/Shankara

It's sort of like Star Wars where you try to become one with the Force, but you also worship a lot of gods on the way.

- *Padmasambhava*—was an eighth-century guru who is said by his followers to have been a totally enlightened being—a Buddha. He is said to have appeared (emanated) as an eight-year-old child and was found sitting on a lotus flower floating on Lake Dhanakosh near the border of Pakistan and India. Though not the first Buddhist to travel to Tibet, he is said to have converted the evil Tibetan gods to Buddhism and founded a monastery there. He is also said to have resided in Tibet for fifty years and in India for 3,600 years.[199] And, his followers say he performed miracles.[200]

Padmasambhava taught there were three realms in the universe—divine, human and demonic.[201] Of himself, he claimed immortality:

No father, no mother, no lineage have I.

Wondrous, I have arisen by myself.

I was never born, and neither shall I die.

I am the Enlightened, I the Lotus-Born.[202]

[199]http://www.muktinath.org/buddhism/padmasambhava.pdf
[200]Yeshe Tsogyal, Erik Pema Kunsang (Translator), *The Lotus-Born: The Life Story of Padamasambhava* (Hong Kong: Rangjung Yeshe Publications, 1998), 3.
[201]http://www.newworldencyclopedia.org/entry/Padmasambhava
[202]Jamgön Mipham, *White Lotus, An Explanation of the Seven-Line Prayer to Guru Padmasambhava* (Boston, MA: Shambhala Publications, 2007), 12.

Padmasambhava taught that eternal ultimate reality (Buddha-nature) exists in each person and it may eventually be experienced as *"the mind evolves and the veils of defilement that conceal the Buddha-nature"* are weakened.[203] For those who don't achieve this experience in this life, many subsequent lives may be needed.

To his followers, Padmasambhava is god-like. They attribute miracles, immortality, and self-existence to him. They even pray to him and have scriptures. How is this not religion?

Sam Harris' mystics taught a mysticism that actually is religion;[204] it comes in a religious wrapper complete with gods, demons, the supernatural, scriptures and a set of defined meditation and prayer practices. It includes polytheism and a form of pantheism all at the same time.

A huge feature within this mysticism is the idea of an **Ultimate Eternal Reality** in which we can all share and that's independent of matter. It existed before matter and us. Yet it seems Sam Harris' mystics are just replacing an eternal personal God with an **eternal thing** that has god-like qualities and of which they make us a part—Ultimate Reality.[205]

---

[203]Ibid., 10.

[204]Merriam-Webster defines **religion** as *"the service and worship of God or the supernatural"* or *"commitment or devotion to religious faith or observance."* https://www.merriam-webster.com/dictionary/religion

[205]**Many Questions:** The teachings of Harris' revered mystics raise a huge number of questions. Here are just a few:

- **Human existence**—If our eternal ultimate self (*Atman*) is the same thing as Ultimate Eternal Reality (*Nirguna Brahman*), did we eternally exist before our own births? Does that make us like a god? If so, why then are we here?
- **Laws**—How did the "law" of reincarnation start? Was this an accident or a decision? What sustains reincarnation now? Does Ultimate Reality have consciousness (mind) apart from us and make decisions apart from us? If so, is this separate ruling consciousness God?
- **Matter**—If we existed before matter, which had a beginning, were we its source and creator or is matter just an illusion? If it is just illusion, how can we all share in the same illusion? If we are not its source, from whence does it come?

IS SAM HARRIS' MYSTICISM EMPIRICAL?

Sam Harris says mysticism is **empirical** and religion isn't. Is he correct? Again, let's start with definitions. Merriam-Webster defines "empirical" as an adjective that generally means "*based on observation or experience.*" [206] Using this first definition, I would agree. Harris' mysticism is empirical in that it is based on a person's subjective observation or experience. However, how would this differ from any other reported religious experience? Using this definition, they're all empirical.

A second definition of empirical is "*capable of being verified or disproven by observation or experiment.*"[207] That means it's testable—this is what Harris claims. Yet, other adherents of the mysticism he praises state that each person may experience enlightenment to ultimate reality differently.[208] How then are subjective mystical experiences testable?

IS SAM HARRIS' MYSTICISM RATIONAL?

It's interesting that Harris calls mysticism **rational**. It's definitely based on thought—it would take at least some thought to develop and communicate these philosophies and religious systems. It also can be rationally discussed.

- **Separation from Ultimate Reality**—What caused people to emanate from Ultimate Reality and become infused into matter in the first place—before birth and the cycle of reincarnation began? Why would we even want to emanate into matter only to strive to return to Ultimate Reality? If we had no choice and something else caused us to emanate into matter, is that "cause" independent of and greater than Ultimate Reality?

[206] https://www.merriam-webster.com/dictionary/empirical
[207] Ibid.
[208] Ngawang Zangpo, *Guru Rinpoché—His Life and Times* (Ithaca, NY: Snow Lion Publications, 2002), 32.

Yet how would this differ from any other philosophical concept, whether they be mystical, religious or not?

MYSTICISM AND ETERNAL EXISTENCE

Unlike other atheists, such as Nietzsche, Bertrand Russell, Richard Dawkins and Stephen Hawking, who say human existence ends at the point of death, it seems what Sam Harris is seeking is eternal existence (eternal life). He just seeks it apart from the existence of God. Let me explain.

Harris acknowledges that we are all conscious beings and his mystics say, when fully enlightened, we can experience nirvana—eternal unity and **eternal existence** with Ultimate Reality. If this is the case, then Ultimate Reality is composed of us and other conscious beings. This would also mean Ultimate Reality isn't just an idea—it's also "ultimate being(s)" who last forever. It makes us all a part of eternal god-like existence without having a God.

CONCLUSION

If all of this is what Harris really believes, it makes little sense for him to say mysticism is rational and religion is not. This mysticism is religion—complete with gods, rituals, prayer, scripture and eternal existence. It just doesn't include a monotheistic Supreme Being.

ALL RELIGION IS MAN-MADE

... the mildest criticism of religion is also the most radical and the most devastating one. Religion is man-made.[209]

—Christopher Hitchens

Christopher Hitchens contended that all religion is man-made. This is a really broad statement, especially for someone who wasn't a theologian or a historian. While well-read, Hitchens wasn't exactly educated or trained in the disciplines that would qualify him as an expert in any religion, much less all of them. His study of philosophy, politics and economics at Oxford may have qualified him as a journalist, social commentator and former Marxist, which he was, but it wouldn't have qualified him as an expert in religion.

---

[209]Christopher Hitchens, *God Is Not Great* (New York: Hachette Book Group, 2007), 10.

What are we to make of Hitchens' claim that all religions are man-made? Let's take a look. Simplistically, there are generally four aspects to any religion: 1) an object of worship, 2) a manner of worship, 3) teachings about deity, and 4) a moral code. If Hitchens is correct that all religion is man-made, then at least the objects of worship and the manner of worship of all religions are the inventions of man. Are they?

- *The object of worship*—In looking at what they worship, it's clear that at least some religions are man-made. Pantheistic, polytheistic and monotheistic religions all have different objects of worship. Though some pluralists might contend otherwise, they can't all be true. They're too different. If there is a God, either everything is God, there is just one God or there are many Gods. At least one of these three groups is mistaken. So, Christopher Hitchens seems to be at least partially correct.
- *The manner of worship*—Most of the people on the planet who believe in God believe there is just one. However, the manner in which they worship that one God can differ. For example, Jews, Christians and Muslims, who all claim to worship the God of Abraham, do so differently. Even among Christians, some of their liturgies and worship practices differ. So, again, Hitchens seems to be at least partially correct. Otherwise, it seems they would all be worshiping in the same way. But do differences always matter? Not necessarily.

Based on just these two aspects of religion, it appears Hitchens is at least partially correct. It seems clear that some objects of worship and some religious practices are man-made. There are too many conflicting claims of deity; too many conflicting claims of revelation from God; too many conflicting religious practices and philosophies. They can't all be true. But can it confidently be said that all of them are man-made? Not really. And, are all divergences in religious practice necessarily meaningful? No.

A broad statement that all religion is man-made **presupposes** there is no God. If this were the case, of course all objects of worship and all manners of worship were invented by people. But can it actually be proven? To attempt to prove that all religion is man-made would at least require a huge team of genuine experts in all religions to decide upon the definitive criteria for evaluating every religion on the planet and then somehow conclusively prove they all fail the test. Good luck with that.

Most of Christopher Hitchens' criticisms of religion aren't actually focused on whether God exists or not. Many of them aren't even core to the religions he attacks. While many of his criticisms are valid, they don't match the breadth of his claim.

Is it **possible** that at least one religion is true? Yes. In the case of monotheism, this would mean it was revealed by God, recognized by man and has practices and morals prescribed in a manner suitable to God. It would not, however, mean that people observe it perfectly. Assuming that people are free moral agents and not puppets, even if the religion they practice is true, they wouldn't necessarily live up to it.

Hitchens' frustration with the teachings and failures of some religions is understandable. However, his extremely broad-brush statement can't be verified. Given this, it doesn't make sense.

MIRACLES CAN'T HAPPEN

If you are that person [who was diagnosed with cancer that then went into remission], *you are more likely to believe that God cured you, this invisible force, creator of the universe, cured you, than that you had three idiotic doctors diagnose you. . . . I taught physics to pre-med students who became doctors. Not all of them are smart, I assure you.*[210]

—Neil deGrasse Tyson

Neil deGrasse Tyson isn't alone among many scientists who are adamant that there is no such thing as miracles. He would rather believe three medical doctors are incompetent than acknowledge the possibility of miracles. However, could it be that the three medical doctors

---

[210]The Amazing Meeting, Keynote Speech, 2008, https://www.youtube.com/playlist?list=PLBDBC78EF8B22B179.

actually got their diagnoses right and the scientist is wrong? How do we resolve the question of the miraculous?

What is a miracle? Let's use two dictionaries this time. The first definition from Merriam-Webster says a miracle is "*an extraordinary event manifesting divine intervention in human affairs.*"[211] The second is from Dictionary.com and says a miracle is "*an effect or extraordinary event in the physical world that surpasses all known human or natural powers and is ascribed to a supernatural cause.*"[212] Between the two definitions, this seems to be what most people mean by miracle.[213]

EVENTS BEYOND KNOWN HUMAN OR NATURAL POWERS?

Starting with Dictionary.com's definition, have there been miracles in nature? Well, yes, there have been many extraordinary events in the physical world that surpass known **natural power** and seem to have a cause which is beyond nature. We've already discussed five of the biggest: a beginning, laws, purposeful information, life and consciousness.

1. *A beginning*—The first extraordinary event that violated the powers of nature was the beginning—the big bang. There was nothing and then there was everything—matter, energy, time, space and precise laws of physics. This was definitely beyond known natural powers, since nature didn't yet exist.

---

[211]https://www.merriam-webster.com/dictionary/miracle?src=search-dict-hed
[212]https://www.dictionary.com/browse/miracle?s=t
[213]Another frequent use of the word "miracle" is to describe an amazing or highly unlikely event without necessarily attributing it to anyone or anything.

2. *Laws*—Laws of physics were present at the beginning. For a system of fine-tuned laws to exist, there had to be a cause (a law giver) and since nature did not exist before its own beginning, nature could not have been the source of its own laws. So, this event was also beyond natural powers.

3. *Purposeful information*—Purposeful information had to exist for the first cell to exist. And this purposeful information had to include instructions for how to self-replicate—or there wouldn't have been a second cell. Physics and chemistry can support life, but they can't provide the information required to start life.

4. *Life*—The next event beyond the powers of nature is the emergence of life from non-life. There is no known law of physics or chemistry that requires life to exist and no known natural process that can cause life to commence.

5. *Consciousness*—Consciousness, self-awareness, thought, the ability to solve and plan, the intellectual ability to build and create—all of these things exist. Many scientists assume they evolved, but they don't know how. It appears, according to Colin McGinn, that the impossible has happened:

> *It appears as if the impossible has occurred. Unconscious physical particles have conspired to generate conscious minds.*[214]

Some atheists state, the fact these things did happen proves they are not miracles. However, that's not true. They might not be miracles if nature could have done them, but nature couldn't have.

---

[214]Colin McGinn, *The Mysterious Flame* (New York: Basic Books, 1999), 15.

McGinn asserts that, while we don't yet know how these things happened, there are answers and, as human intellect grows, we'll ultimately figure it out.[215] Whether this is wishful thinking or not is to be seen. However, right now, we have no clue as to how these things happened. They're beyond any known law or process in nature. They're the big leaps that surpass known *natural powers*. According to the Dictionary.com definition, they're miracles.

EXTRAORDINARY EVENTS IN HUMAN AFFAIRS?

Now on to human affairs. What about Merriam-Webster's definition? Have there been extraordinary events that suggest *divine intervention in human affairs?* To answer this question, history is a place to look. Has God intervened in human history? Both Judaism and Christianity claim the answer is yes.[216] Other religions make this claim as well. Are these claims true?

- *Judaism*—A big claim of Judaism is that God is real and that he promised Abraham, Isaac and Jacob (Israel) to be their God and to bless them so they could then be a blessing to the entire world—forever.[217] The fact is, about 4,000 years later, Israel and the Jewish people still exist. And, Jews, who don't even comprise 2/10ths of one percent of the world's population, have had a massively disproportionate

---

[215]Michael Shermer with Colin McGinn – "Mysterianism, Consciousness, Free Will & God," July 16, 2018, https://www.youtube.com/watch?v=twrQk-eF2r4.

[216]Reform Judaism and some liberal Christian denominations may deny the occurrence of miracles. However, the overwhelming majority of Jewish and Christian denominations believe God has and still does intervene in human affairs.

[217]Genesis 12:1-3, Genesis 17:19-22, Genesis 26:24-25, Genesis 28:1-5, Genesis 32:22-30,

influence on the world in business, entertainment, medicine, science and education. That seems sort of miraculous.

- *Christianity*—A big claim of Christianity is that Jesus said he was going to be executed and he would then rise from the dead three days later.[218] Now that would definitely be a miracle. Yet, his first-century followers claim this is actually what happened.[219] Were they telling the truth? After evaluating first-century witness accounts, J. Warner Wallace, a detective and expert in forensic statement analysis, concluded they were. To him, their testimony was so credible that he changed his own position from atheism to theism.[220]

What about today? Are there reported interventions of God in our daily lives? Yes. Are all of them real? Probably not. After all, not everything attributed even to people, both good and bad, is always true or accurate. But could many of these accounts be true?

About 79 percent of Americans believe in miracles. That's true of both millennials and older Americans. Are they correct?[221] How would you prove or test reported miracles? In many cases, you likely can't. There are often other possible explanations—you were just misdiagnosed (as Neil deGrasse Tyson suggests), the job offer was just a coincidence, you were just lucky to survive the fall, and so on.

---

[218] Mark 8:31; 9:30–32; 10:32–34; Matthew 12:39–40; John 2:19–22

[219] Matthew 27:57–28:20; Mark 15:41–16:20; Luke 23:50–53; John 19:38–21:25; 2 Peter 1:16

[220] J. Warner Wallace, *Cold-Case Christianity: A Homicide Detective Investigates the Claims of the Gospels* (Colorado Springs: David C. Cook, 2013), 18.

[221] *Millennial Generation Less Religiously active than Older Americans* (Washington, DC: Pew Research Center, 2010), https://www.pewforum.org/2010/02/17/millennial-generation-less-religiously-active-than-older-americans/

If "miracles" can't often be conclusively proven, why then do most Americans believe miracles occur? After all, unlikely things do actually happen from time to time—people do win the lottery and they also get struck by lightning.

Whether because of perceived improbability of natural causes, incredible timing, correlation with prayer or other reasons, many people infer to the most logical conclusion. To them, a logical conclusion is divine intervention. In many cases, these conclusions are supported by hard evidence. In others, they're not.

It's clear that there have been significant events in nature that exceed the laws of nature. Even scientists and philosophers who are atheists call them "miraculous." There have also been credible events in human history that have been attributed to divine intervention. And, most Americans believe that miracles either occur or are possible.

Given this, what doesn't make sense is the perspective that miracles don't happen **because** miracles don't happen. After all, isn't it more likely that three trained medical doctors who agree on a patient's dire diagnosis and miraculous recovery are correct than it is that one scientist who disagrees is?

CHRISTIANITY

JESUS MAY OR MAY NOT HAVE EXISTED

Historically it is quite doubtful whether
Christ ever existed at all, and if He did we do
not know anything about Him . . .[222]

—Bertrand Russell

Bertrand Russell, perhaps the most famous atheist of the post–World War II generation, suggested Jesus' existence was *"quite doubtful."* Christopher Hitchens, in his tirade titled, *god Is Not Great*, asserted that Jesus' existence was *"highly questionable."*[223] Richard Dawkins, a bit more charitably, says Jesus probably existed.[224] These are rather surprising statements from such educated people.

---

[222]Bertrand Russell, *Why I Am Not a Christian* (New York: Simon & Schuster, 1957), 16.
[223]Christopher Hitchens, *God Is Not Great* (New York: Hachette Book Group, 2009), 114.
[224]Richard Dawkins, *The God Delusion* (New York: Houghton Mifflin Harcourt, 2008), 122.

Stating that Jesus of Nazareth **probably** existed is sort of like saying Pontus Pilate or King Herod probably existed. Most historians would consider that to be an uninformed statement. Of course he existed. However, to humor Dawkins, Hitchens and Russell, let's ask the question anyway—did a Jewish person called Jesus of Nazareth really live in Israel (the Kingdom of Judea) in the first century and, more specifically, did his followers consider him to be the Jewish Messiah?

Let's start with Flavius Josephus, a Jewish historian who was really close to the events in the Kingdom of Judea (Israel) in the first century. He was a general in the Jewish army that unsuccessfully revolted against the Roman Empire in 66 AD. He had quite a bit to say about Jesus:

> At this time there was a wise man who was called Jesus. His conduct was good, and [he] was known to be virtuous. And many people from among the Jews and the other nations became his disciples. Pilate condemned him to be crucified and to die. But those who had become his disciples did not abandon his discipleship. They reported that he had appeared to them three days after his crucifixion and that he was alive; accordingly, he was perhaps the Messiah, concerning whom the prophets have recounted wonders.

—Josephus, *Antiquities of the Jews*, (18.3.3)[225]

According to Josephus, not only did Jesus really exist, so did John the Baptist, King Herod, Festus, Felix, Agrippa,

---

[225] Shlomo Pines, *An Arabic Version of the Testimonium Flavium and Its Implications* (Jerusalem: Jerusalem Academic Press, 1971), 9–10.

This translation of a tenth-century Arabic manuscript is neutral toward Jesus being the Messiah. Other ancient manuscripts explicitly state he is the Messiah.

Pontius Pilate, James (the half-brother of Jesus) and lots of other people written about in the *New Testament*. Flavius Josephus wrote about all of them in his histories—because they were real people.[226]

Now let's look at what Tacitus, a first-century Roman historian, had to say. He recorded that Emperor Nero (AD 54–68) blamed the fire that destroyed much of the city of Rome on the Christians and had them sadistically executed in large numbers. He further conveyed that the name Christian came from *"Christus"* who *"had been executed during the rule of Tiberius by the procurator Pontius Pilate."*[227]

Suetonius, an early second-century Roman historian conveyed that the Jews in Rome were in such an uproar about a *"Chrestus,"* that Emperor Claudius (AD 41–54) expelled them from the city.[228] He also conveyed that Emperor Domitian (AD 81–96) killed a cousin who was *"thought by some to have been a convert to the Christian religion."*[229]

Pliny the Younger, a first-century Roman governor of Bithynia-Pontus (in Asia Minor), inquired in a letter to Emperor Trajan (AD 98–117) about how Christians should be treated. He wanted to know whether his practice of arresting and torturing Christians to recant and curse Christ and then executing those who didn't was to be standard practice. In his letter, he conveyed that Christians

> . . . *were accustomed to assemble at dawn on a fixed day, to sing a hymn antiphonally to Christ as God, and to bind themselves by an oath, not for the commission of some crime, but to avoid acts of theft, brigandage, and adultery, not to*

---

[226]Flavius Josephus, *Wars of the Jews* and *Antiquities of the Jews*.

[227] Tacitus, *Annals*, 359.

[228] Suetonius, *Lives of the Twelve Caesars*, 228.

[229] Suetonius, 359.

break their word, and not to withhold money deposited with them when asked for it.[230]

What about the Jewish religious leaders who didn't accept Jesus as the Jewish Messiah? As you might expect, they wrote about him too. Their contentions about Jesus were recorded in the Talmud, which was compiled in the centuries after Jesus' death. It attributed Jesus' miracles to sorcery and conveyed that Jesus was executed for blasphemy. And, because Jesus was *"connected with the government"* (or the kingship), a herald announced for forty days that he would be executed. The Talmud records that his execution occurred just before the Jewish Passover.[231]

It seems odd that Jewish and Roman sources, who weren't even followers of Jesus, would record these incidents from Jesus' life, if he weren't a real person. Yet, according to them, Jesus of Nazareth really lived. He was a first-century Jew who was seen as virtuous, deemed to have performed miracles and was regarded as the Messiah (the Christ) by many.

His theological opponents saw his miracles as sorcery, accused him of blasphemy and sought his execution. He was crucified just before the Jewish Passover by Pontius Pilate, the Roman governor of Judea, (AD 26–36) during the reign of Tiberius Caesar. Jesus' followers then claimed they saw him alive three days after his crucifixion and worshiped him as God. His followers also sought to live virtuous lives and came to be called Christians.

All these things can be easily established from sources who were not Jesus' followers. We'll save another source for the next chapter.

---

[230] Pliny The Younger, Complete *Letters* (New York: Oxford University Press, 2006), 278–79.
[231] *Babylonian Talmud*, Tractate Sanhedrin (43a), (London: Soncino Press, 1987).

THE GOSPELS ARE UNRELIABLE

*Well, it can be stated with certainty, and on
their own evidence, that the Gospels are most
certainly not literal truth.*[232]

—Christopher Hitchens

Why would atheists care whether the Gospels, the
accounts of Jesus' life, are accurate or not? The
answer seems obvious—if the Gospel accounts are accurate, there is a God. However, if they are not, the stories
about Jesus are just misguided legends.

There seem to be four options when it comes to the
historicity of the accounts of Jesus' life. They are either fiction, historical novels, inaccurate historical accounts or
accurate historical accounts. Let's look at each option:

1. *Fiction*—The four accounts of Jesus' life could have
   been made up—they could be total fiction. However,

---

[232]Christopher Hitchens, *God Is Not Great*, 120.

it's clear that at least many of the people, events and places mentioned were real. There really was a Roman Emperor named Caesar Augustus. There really was a governor of the Roman province of Judea named Pontus Pilate. There really were people named John the Baptist, Herod the Great and Jesus. There really was a Jewish Temple in Jerusalem and Jewish sects called Pharisees and Sadducees. Josephus, the first-century Jewish historian ,wrote about all of them.[233] So, the Gospels were definitely not total fiction. At least much of what they record is real and true.

2. *Historical novel*—Another option is that the Gospels were a historical novel—sort of like the novel *Gone with the Wind*—a fictional story placed in a real historical setting. While this is possible, the key people and events of Jesus' life are easily verified by independent sources. For example, Josephus confirms that Jesus was thought to be the Messiah, he was crucified by Pontus Pilate and his followers thought he rose from the dead. Jesus' life clearly isn't just a novel set in history, but is it accurate history?

3. *Historical accounts but inaccurate*—If the story of Jesus' life isn't fiction, maybe it's just an embellished story of a real person named Jesus. Or perhaps it is a real story that's just inaccurate. If either of these were the case, the four different authors of the four Gospels would have had to coordinate the embellishments or made the same mistakes. While not impossible, it would be difficult.

If the stories of Jesus' life are coordinated embellishments, the writers did a great job. There actually is

---

[233]Josephus, *Antiquities of the Jews* and *Wars of the Jews*

remarkable consistency in their accounts of events.[234] And, not only is there consistency between accounts, there is historical accuracy. It seems Luke, one of the Gospel writers, is deemed to have been one of the world's great historians. The eminent archaeologist Sir William Ramsey said Luke is *"a historian of first rank; not merely are his statements of fact trustworthy . . . this author should be placed along with the greatest of historians."*[235] This is a remarkable statement, if Luke was just a liar.

Consistent, historically accurate accounts wouldn't have been expected if the authors—fishermen, a tax collector and a medical doctor—were just making up a fable.

4. *Historical accounts and accurate*—A final option is that the historical events the writers of the four Gospels recorded are accurate.

Celsus, a second-century Greek philosopher, wrote an extensive refutation of the claims of Christianity titled True Discourse.[236] In it, he readily conceded the fact that Jesus really lived, saying, "a few years ago he began to teach this doctrine, being regarded by Christians as the son of God."[237] However, he sought to refute the claims of Jesus' virgin birth, miracles and resurrection from the dead.

---

[234]F.F. Bruce, *The New Testament Documents: Are They Reliable?* (Downers Grove, IL, Intervarsity Press, 1960), 31.

[235]William M. Ramsay, *The Bearing of Recent Discovery on the Trustworthiness of the New Testament* (Grand Rapids: Baker Book House, 1953), 222.

[236]The contents of Celsus' *True Discourse* have been reconstructed through a detailed argument by argument rebuttal written by Origen, entitled *Against Celsus*.

[237]Origen, *Against Celsus*, Alexander Roberts & James Donaldson, *Ante-Nicene Fathers*, Vol. 4 (Peabody, MA: Hendrickson, 1999), 407.

He attributed Jesus' parentage to a Roman soldier, his miracles to sorcery and magic, and his resurrection to a shadow.[238] Celsus acknowledged Jesus' suffering and death, calling it *"punishment by the Jews for his crimes."*[239] He called Jesus' apostles *"tax-gatherers and sailors of the vilest character."*[240]

On balance, Celsus didn't seek to deny that Jesus lived, taught, performed miracles or was crucified and died. He didn't even deny the reports of Jesus' resurrection from the dead. What he did seek to do was attribute a miraculous birth to natural means, other miracles to magic, and a resurrection to a shadow. Yet, all the while, Celsus was a polytheist, embracing the pantheon of Greek gods.

Celsus clearly believed in the gods. He also acknowledged that Jesus was real and the basic events recorded in the Gospels were historical, he just didn't believe in the God of the Jews, that Jesus' life was miraculous, or that Jesus was God incarnate. His primary problem with Christians wasn't the basic historicity of Jesus' life. He had a problem with attributing the events of Jesus' life to God—especially when that God wasn't Greek.

Where does this leave us? It seems the people who lived during and shortly after Jesus' earthly life, who observed or heard about him, fell into two categories. Some observed or attributed the events of Jesus' life to God and believed he was, in fact, the son of God. Others attributed the reported miracles and resurrection to other things. However, the historicity of Jesus and the basic events of his life were not seen as the primary question.

---

[238]Origen, *Against Celsus*, 410, 399, 427, 472.
[239]Origen, *Against Celsus*, 420, 431, 448.
[240]Origen, *Against Celsus*, 424.

Given the evidence available, it doesn't make sense to attack the reliability of the accounts of the basic events of Jesus' life. The key thing in question is whether the Gospel writers were correct in attributing these events to miracles and ascribing Jesus with divinity.

JESUS' MORALITY IS TOO MORAL

The order to "love thy neighbor" is mild and yet stern: a reminder of one's duty to others. The order to "love thy neighbor as thyself" is too extreme and too strenuous to be obeyed, as is the hard to interpret instruction to love others "as I have loved you." Humans are not so constituted as to care for others as much as themselves: the thing simply cannot be done . . .[241]

—Christopher Hitchens

C hristopher Hitchens made many comments about religion during his life. In fact, his book, *god is not Great,* is not so much about whether God exists as it is an expression of his deep-felt displeasure with religion. As previously mentioned, some of the critical things he said about religion were accurate. Others were not. Yet others, such

---

[241]Hitchens, *God Is Not Great,* 213.

as this quotation about Jesus' morality, showed his lack of a real understanding of the religions to which he took exception.

It's true Jesus' moral code exceeded the normal conduct of people in both the first century and the twenty-first century. That's because moral standards aren't based on what the average person does; they're based on what truly moral conduct is. Truly moral conduct is loving, truthful, faithful, good, pure and just to everyone—even people who don't like us.[242] It's based on the conviction that every person has value and they should be treated that way. That's how we should seek to live. Will we always succeed? No. But, we shouldn't lower the bar just to make ourselves feel better.

Jesus also gave people two simple ways to know what to do in any given situation. After all, treating others well isn't just about a list of 613 moral laws. We experience unique situations every day.

The first general moral principle was to love (or treat) other people the way you would like to be loved.[243] This was taught by both Judaism and Jesus. The second was to love people the way Jesus did. He said his own life was to serve as an example of how to treat others.[244]

Was Jesus' moral code impossible? Was it too moral? Based upon what we see in life every day, the answer is no. We see parents loving their children selflessly. We see soldiers laying down their lives to defend others. We see billionaires giving away half of their possessions so others can live better lives. We see selfless love, compassion, and the pursuit of justice for others every day. While this kind of behavior isn't always the norm, people do these things all the time.

---

[242]Matthew 5:43–48
[243]Matthew 19:17–19; 22:34–40
[244]John 13:34–35; 15:9–13

Instead of lowering the bar of what is moral, Judaism and Christianity state that God will forgive our moral failures.[245] Christianity even takes it one step further and emphasizes that God offers us his moral purity.[246] Yet forgiveness is not seen by either faith as a "pass" to behave immorally.

Another observation is, in claiming Jesus' moral code is *too strenuous to be obeyed*," Hitchens is inadvertently giving Christianity support for Jesus' divinity. If no mere mortal could have a moral code like Jesus', what does that say about Jesus?

It seems Hitchens missed the point of what Judaism and Christianity actually teach. Given this, his comment makes no sense.

---

[245]Psalm 103:8–18; Isaiah 52:13–53:12; 1 John 1:8–10

[246]Christianity teaches that Jesus (God incarnate) bore the guilt and punishment for human moral failure and offers humanity forgiveness, pardon, "righteousness" and help in living morally. (Romans 3:21–26; Philippians 3:7–9; 1:9–11; 2:12–13)

ATHEISTS
FOR JESUS

Atheists for Jesus.

—Richard Dawkins

This is actually one of the more surprising statements to come from an atheist and it actually occurred. In about 2006, Richard Dawkins wrote an essay titled *Atheists for Jesus*. In this essay, he complimented Jesus' moral code as being higher than that of first-century Judaism:

> *At least in the teachings that are attributed to him, he* [Jesus] *publicly advocated niceness and was one of the first to do so.*[247]

In pondering this and several other statements Dawkins has made, it seems he wants to have it both ways—he praises Jesus' morality, but states that Jesus may not have even existed. He says Jesus possessed a high intellect, but that

---

[247]Richard Dawkins, *Atheists for Jesus*, https://www.rationalresponders.com/atheists_for_jesus_ a_richard_dawkins_essay.

he didn't actually consider himself to be God. He relies on the Gospel accounts to reach conclusions about Jesus' life but says the accounts are unreliable. [248] This inconsistency doesn't make sense.

Richard Dawkins isn't alone in making inconsistent statements. Citing events from the Gospel accounts of Jesus' life, Bertrand Russell also stated that Jesus possessed *"a very high degree of moral goodness."* Then, a few pages later, he questioned Jesus' existence and stated that nothing is known about him. [249] Yet if nothing is known about Jesus, how could Russell conclude that Jesus was highly moral?

It's obvious that atheists admire the attributes Jesus displayed in the Gospel accounts of his life—morality, intellect and compassion. However, C. S. Lewis, a professor at Oxford and Cambridge Universities, [250] pointed out that Jesus can't merely be regarded as a highly moral person or as highly intelligent. Doing so makes no sense.

Lewis highlighted that if Jesus was highly moral, then he wasn't a liar. If Jesus was intelligent, he likely wasn't crazy. And, if Jesus wasn't a liar or crazy, he must be who he claimed to be—God. Jesus didn't really leave us with the option of accepting him as less. [251] For about 33 percent of the people on planet Earth, this is the conclusion they have reached.

---

[248]The following question is also worth considering. If Jesus didn't exist, how could his followers—four fishermen, a tax collector, and a bunch of other average guys—have invented a character called Jesus whose demonstrated moral code and intellect was superior to theirs?

[249]Bertrand Russell, *Why I Am Not a Christian* (New York: Simon & Schuster, 1957), 5, 16.

[250]C. S. Lewis, a professor of English Literature during the 1920s through the 1960s, was one of the most famous Christian apologists of the twentieth century.

[251]C. S. Lewis, *Mere Christianity* (New York: HarperOne, 2001), 52–53.

DEATH

"WHEN I DIE
I SHALL ROT"

*. . . I believe that when I die I shall rot, and
nothing of my ego will survive.*[252]

—Bertrand Russell

Is there finality in death? Most atheists think so. Bertrand
Russell certainly did. His expectation was that his body
would rot, his consciousness would end, and that would
be the end of him. Was he correct? How would we know?
It seems that most dead people aren't very talkative about
their experiences.

The key question is whether your consciousness (call it
your soul) will survive after your body ages and dies. Bertrand Russell thought the body and soul were indivisible
and any notion that they are not was *"metaphysical
superstition."*[253] He was open to considering new research
results and to changing his mind, if new evidence justified

---

[252]Bertrand Russell, "What I Believe" in *Why I Am Not a Christian* (New York:
Simon & Schuster, 1957), 54.
[253]Ibid., 52.

doing so. However, based on what was known in the 1950s, it seemed logical to him that when your body is dead, all of you is dead. You are not immortal.

It seems medicine has advanced a lot since the 1950s. While the phenomenon of people being resuscitated after death was known then, even more people are now surviving death. Many people whose hearts and brain functions have stopped and were considered clinically dead have been resuscitated. This is a big deal.

In 1975, Raymond Moody, a PhD in philosophy and psychology, authored a book titled *Life After Life*. It caused a stir because it presented the results of interviews with people who had been declared clinically dead and were then resuscitated.

Since then, there have been several other similar books and TV shows, like *I Survived . . . Beyond and Back*, which present interviews with people who reportedly survived death experiences.[254] These people claim their consciousness didn't end when they were declared dead. Many even claimed to have experienced heaven.

Multiple scientific studies support these claims.

- *England*—A study in 2014 of 2,060 people who had died of cardiac arrest was performed by researchers at the University of Southampton in England. Of the 330 who were resuscitated, 140 participated in their survey. Of these, 39 percent said they were aware while they were being resuscitated by doctors and 13 percent *"felt separated from their bodies."* [255]

---

[254]http://www.mylifetime.com/movies/i-survived-beyond-and-back
[255]Sarah Knapton, *First hint of 'life after death' in biggest ever scientific study*, Telegraph, (London, England: Telegraph Media Group Ltd., October 7, 2014), http://www.telegraph.co.uk/science/2016/03/12/first-hint-of-life-after-death-in-biggest-ever-scientific-study/

- *America*—Researchers often call incidents where people died and were later resuscitated *near death experiences* (NDEs). An analysis by researchers at the Division of Perceptual Studies, located at the University of Virginia, revealed that 42 percent of people experiencing NDEs reported encountering other people who were deceased during their NDE, including people they didn't know. Many others reported having out-of-body experiences where they saw things from a distance that were subsequently verified as factual. [256]

Do these people's experiences *prove* that consciousness continues after the point of physical death? Not conclusively. However, they provide substantial evidence that it does. If this is the case, it's also evidence to support the existence of God. After all, if people can consciously exist apart from physical matter (their bodies), God can too.

Would Bertrand Russell have changed his mind, based upon this new research? Perhaps or perhaps not. But, it certainly wouldn't make sense to ignore it.

If our conscious soul continues to exist after death, the existence of God is worthy of some investigation. After all, we might just end up meeting him.

---

[256]Edward F. Kelly, Emily Williams Kelly, et al., *Irreducible Mind: Toward a Psychology for the 21st Century* (New York: Rowan & Littlefield Publishers, Inc., 2007), 390, 400.

WHAT WOULD NATURE SUGGEST ABOUT A GOD?

A ntony Flew, a philosopher, thought about the question of God's existence for fifty years and during that time, was emphatic that God did not exist. Then he changed his mind. The new evidence, which ultimately was compelling to him, wasn't religious or theological—it was scientific. He found recent discoveries about the universe and DNA to be convincing. Nature changed his mind.

Flew saw atheism as his logical starting position. However, he was open to hearing evidence that might support the case for God. He maintained that if adequate evidence was presented, he would change his mind. He was adamant that his conclusions would be based only on what science and reason could reveal. Then, after almost a lifetime of assessing the information available, he concluded:

> I have followed the argument where it has led me. And it has led me to accept the existence of a self-existent, immutable, immaterial, omnipotent, and omniscient Being.[257]

---

[257] Antony Flew, *There Is a God* (New York: HarperCollins, 2007), 155.

This statement sent a shock wave through the atheist world. Had he lost his senses? He assured the world he had not.

It's noteworthy that, in addition to stating that he accepted the existence of God, Antony Flew presented his views as to what God must logically be like. Based on science, this is what he concluded:

- *Self-existent*—Since the universe had a beginning and since nature cannot logically create itself out of nothing, there had to be a self-existent first-cause.[258]
- *Immaterial*—The self-existent first-cause could not be subject to nature or the laws of nature, which themselves came into existence at the same moment matter, energy, space and time did. Therefore, God is not composed of matter[259]—at least not as we know it—and exists beyond space and time.
- *Immutable*—Constant laws of nature suggest a God who is not fickle and is unchangeable.[260]
- *Omnipotent*—For God to have been the source of all that exists, God would have to possess the power to make it happen. Since this power exceeds the energy in the universe, God is all-powerful.
- *Omnipresent*—A self-existent immaterial God, would not be limited by the physical and would be all-present.[261]
- *Omniscient*—The fine-tuned laws of physics, the information and programs found in DNA and purpose in biological systems caused Flew to conclude that the universe and life were designed. Therefore, God knows everything there is to know.[262]

---

[258]Ibid.
[259]Ibid., 111–12, 151–54.
[260]Ibid., 109–12.
[261]Ibid., 155.
[262]Ibid., 132.

- *Being*—The design and purpose found in the universe suggested to Flew that God possesses intelligence. Therefore, God must be a Being, not an impersonal force or a thing.[263]
- *Eternal*—Flew reasoned, "*If anything at all exists, there must be something preceding it that always existed.*" This was either God or the universe.[264] Since the universe had a beginning, it had to be God.
- *Purpose*—For an all-powerful, all-knowing, self-existent being to **decide** to create the universe, there would have been a reason. The universe and the things in it would not have been an accident nor would they be necessary. [265] If God had a purpose for creating the universe, there must still be a purpose for its existence and there is a purpose for our existence as well.

If Antony Flew was correct, there is at least one more thing this would suggest about God.

- *Goodness*—If God is self-existent, he doesn't really need us to exist; he isn't dependent upon us to make him God. So, he wants us to exist. The fact that we are not robots or zombies suggests that God is good enough to grant us real choices as real beings.

Though Antony Flew didn't provide an answer, we are left to wonder why a God would **want** other volitional beings to exist. After all, if God exists and he doesn't need us, why bother creating us?

---

[263] Ibid., 88, 149.
[264] Ibid., 165.
[265] Ibid., 107–8.

It may be that a friend's six-year-old daughter had the right idea. She asked him why God made people. As he fumbled for an answer she might grasp, she answered her own question. "*I know!*" she said. "*God just wanted children to love.*"

Perhaps she's right.

ATHEISTS WHO CHANGED THEIR MINDS

You may find the ideas presented in this book to be a lot to process. Take your time. Others have asked the same questions, considered the evidence available and reached their conclusions in much the same way you have or will. However, as you ponder these ideas, it may be helpful to hear the stories of ten people who also thought a lot about whether God exists. They are former atheists who changed their minds.

Including these people's stories certainly doesn't prove that God exists. That's not the intent. The intent is, through their stories, to reveal why they rejected what was, in many cases, a very strongly held position.

What's readily apparent in reading these stories is that the people selected are intelligent. They weren't duped into accepting theism or deism and they didn't casually change their minds. They all had reasons for concluding that there is a God.

It's also apparent that the evidence they assessed was broad and included several topics not covered in this book—mathematics, beauty, music, art and personal experience.

Their reasons were different, but their conclusion was the same.

I hope you find their stories to be insightful.

ALISTER MCGRATH

Alister McGrath is an interesting man. He grew up in Northern Ireland in the 1950s and 1960s, was an accomplished student, and earned a scholarship to study chemistry at Oxford University. And, like many other smart students at the time, he concluded that intelligent people don't believe in God:

> *When I was growing up in Belfast, Northern Ireland, during the 1960s, I came to the view that God was an infantile illusion, suitable for the elderly, the intellectually feeble, and the fraudulently religious. I admit this was a rather arrogant view, and one that I now find somewhat embarrassing. My rather pathetic excuse for this intellectual haughtiness is that a lot of other people felt the same way back then. It was the received wisdom of the day that religion was on its way out, and that a glorious, godless dawn was just around the corner.*[266]

It was while studying chemistry at Oxford that McGrath realized science answers many questions well, but it doesn't answer questions related to **purpose, meaning and identity**. These deeper questions that science couldn't answer caused McGrath to explore Christianity. He concluded that a

---

[266]http://www.beliefnet.com/news/science-religion/2005/08/breaking-the-science-atheism-bond.aspx

theistic view made more sense of human existence than the atheism he had previously embraced.[267]

McGrath has since earned three doctoral degrees at Oxford University: a PhD in molecular biophysics, a DD in theology and a DLitt in humanities for research in the history of ideas related to science and religion. He's an Oxford professor and has written a rebuttal of the atheistic views of his Oxford colleague, Richard Dawkins.

FRANCIS COLLINS

Francis Collins is a scientist's scientist. He earned a PhD in physical chemistry at Yale and an MD at the University of North Carolina. As a faculty researcher at the University of Michigan, he helped identify the genes responsible for neurofibromatosis, cystic fibrosis and Huntington's disease. As the head of the international Human Genome Project, he coordinated the efforts of thousands of genetic scientists globally as they completed the mapping and sequencing of human DNA. He is now the head of the U.S. National Institutes of Health. That's a scientist.

Francis Collins also believes in God, though that hasn't always been the case. While a twenty-six-year-old student at UNC's School of Medicine and an atheist, it was the existence of **moral law** that opened him to the possibility of God's existence. It seemed to him:

> *What we have here is very peculiar: the concept of right and wrong appears to be universal among all members of the human species (though its application may result in wildly different*

---

[267] Alister McGrath, *The Twilight of Atheism* (Colorado Springs, CO: WaterBrook Press, 2004), 175-179.

outcomes). It thus seems to be a phenomenon approaching that of a law, like the law of gravitation or of special relativity.[268]

The universality of moral law caused Collins to ponder its source. Was it random? Was it biological? Was it a global coincidence? It seemed a logical *possibility* to him that its source is God. And, ultimately, that's the conclusion he reached. However, while the existence of moral law was compelling to Collins, it wasn't moral law alone that convinced him of God's existence. He also saw the **big bang, the expansion of the universe, order in creation** and **mathematics** as solid evidence.[269] After assessing these factors, Collins concluded:

> *I had started this journey of intellectual exploration to confirm my atheism. That now lay in ruins as the argument from the Moral Law (and many other issues) forced me to admit the plausibility of the God hypothesis. Agnosticism, which had seemed like a safe second-place haven, now loomed like the great cop-out it often is. Faith in God now seemed more rational than disbelief.*[270]

ANTONY FLEW

Antony Flew was an Oxford University educated philosopher and a professor of philosophy at universities in England, Canada and the United States. He described himself

---

[268]Francis Collins, *The Language of God* (New York: Free Press, 2007), 23.

[269] Ibid., 67, 71–75, 93.

[270] Ibid., 30.

as having been the *"world's most notorious atheist"*[271] and he likely was. Commencing with his famous essay *Theology and Falsification* in 1950 and for the following five decades, he was one of the world's leading advocates of atheistic humanism. In fact, he even wrote the book Atheistic Humanism in 1993.

Though Flew was the son of a Methodist minister and attended a Methodist boarding school, he embraced atheism at an early age. He conveyed the impact that traveling to Germany had on him as a child just before World War II and stated, *"One of those early reasons for my conversion to atheism was the problem of evil."*[272] Flew also embraced Marxist communism, which holds to atheism as a core tenet. He later rejected Marxism but held to atheism.

As a philosopher and an atheist, Flew seemed to stack the deck against people who believe in God. He began his case for atheism by contending the starting point should be that *atheism is valid until proven otherwise.*[273] He asserted, from this position, it's then necessary to:

1. Prove there was an originating and then sustaining cause to the Universe,
2. Determine whether that cause is personal, and then,
3. Determine whether that cause is good.[274]

By doing this, he placed the burden for proving the existence of God on deists and theists and asserted that atheists have no responsibility to disprove God.

Then, in 2004, after fifty years of being one of atheism's most vocal advocates, Antony Flew changed his mind and announced:

---

[271] Antony Flew, *There Is a God* (New York: HarperCollins, 2007), 1.

[272] Ibid., 13.

[273] Ibid., 23.

[274] Ibid., 25.

*I now believe that the universe was brought into
existence by an infinite Intelligence. I believe that
this universe's intricate laws manifest what scientists have called the Mind of God. I believe that
life and reproduction originate in a divine
Source.*[275]

What happened? How did such a long-time ardent atheist
change his mind?

Since he was an atheist for five decades, it took much
more than just one thing for Antony Flew to change his
mind. His U-turn started by revisiting two of his own philosophical assumptions, which he then rejected.[276] He was
also immensely influenced by scientific discoveries:

- *The laws of nature*—Flew observed that incredibly
  precise laws of nature exist, but don't exist because
  anything in nature requires them to do so.[277]
- *A fine-tuned universe*—He saw the *"profusion"* of
  cases where the universe is fine-tuned and observed,
  *"the laws of nature seem to have been crafted so as
  to move the universe toward the emergence and sus-
  tenance of life."* [278]
- *DNA evidence*—DNA was crucial evidence to support the existence of God. He concluded that purposeful self-replicating living organisms which

---

[275]Ibid., 88.
[276]Flew rejected David Hume's views that there was no basis for accepting the concept of cause and effect and natural law. Flew concluded: "*Hume was utterly wrong
to maintain that we have no experience, and hence no genuine ideas, of making
things happen and of preventing things from happening, of physical necessity and
physical impossibility.*" Flew also rejected his earlier belief that choices weren't genuine and were merely physically caused. He concluded that choices are genuine.
[277]Flew, *There Is a God*, 98, 107, 111.
[278]Ibid., 114–15.

operate genetic coded programs using stored information suggests an intelligent cause—a Creator.[279]

- *Organisms with purpose*—Flew bent to and then accepted the idea that because living matter has purpose and reproduces and non-living matter does not, it brings into question the idea that nature itself brought life into existence.[280]
- *Biogenesis' inadequacy*—He also observed that theories of chemical evolution were inadequate to explain the existence of genetic code.[281]
- *The big bang*—Flew reversed his position on the big bang and accepted it as evidence for God. He reasoned that nature couldn't have come about from nothing and, at the same time, from a preexisting law of nature requiring it do so. It had to have a cause from outside of nature.[282]

Antony Flew, the philosopher, accepted the existence of God primarily based upon scientific evidence. He said his was not a religious pilgrimage; it was "*a pilgrimage of reason and not of faith*."[283] He then saw himself as a deist in the same sense Aristotle was and didn't accept any specific religion. He was evaluating religions before his death in 2010 and saw Christianity as the front-runner.

SARAH SALVIANDER

As a child, Sarah Salviander was enthralled by outer space. The original *Star Wars* movie trilogy and the television

---

[279]Ibid., 124.
[280]Ibid., 125–26.
[281]Ibid., 128–29.
[282]Ibid., 141–45.
[283]Ibid., 93.

shows *Star Trek* and *Cosmos* captured her imagination and her ambition. She was hooked. By the age of nine, she knew she wanted to be a space scientist. A few decades later, with a PhD in astrophysics in hand, she was.

Sarah Salviander was born in the U.S. but spent most of her early life in western Canada. While there, she grew up without any religious influence. Her parents were atheists, though they preferred to be called agnostics. And, even in the 1970s, western Canada was very non-religious.

By her mid-twenties, Sarah had only met three people who claimed to be Christians. Yet, even without direct exposure to people who believed in God, Sarah was hostile toward Christianity. It was the general attitude of the people around her. To Sarah, Christianity merely *"made people weak and foolish."* She saw it as *"philosophically trivial."*[284]

Rather than embracing her parents' socialism, Sarah embraced the personal independence she saw in **objectivism**. It's the philosophy espoused by Russian novelist Ayn Rand. It is atheistic, capitalistic, sees selfishness as a virtue and describes personal happiness as the highest moral value.[285]

However, while in college, she discarded objectivism. She saw it as cold and impersonal and unable to answer the bigger questions of life related to existence and purpose. Besides, she was consumed by the new intellectual challenges of physics and mathematics.

Sarah attended college in Oregon. It was there, for the first time in her life, that she actually became acquainted with Christians. A few were physics professors whom she respected. Because of them, her hostility toward people

---

[284]Sarah Salviander, *My Testimony*, SixDay Science, May 11, 2019, https://sixday-science.com/2015/05/11/my-testimony/.
[285]Ayn Rand, *The Virtue of Selfishness* (New York: Signet Books, 1964), 30.

who believe in God began to wane. However, it wasn't until her sophomore year, while doing a summer research internship, that her own ideas about God changed.

At the University of California - San Diego's Center for Astrophysics and Space Sciences, Sarah was part of a team researching evidence for the big bang by studying the amount of deuterium (a hydrogen isotope) in the early life of our universe. What astonished her was that you can even do this. She was amazed the universe is so comprehensible. She was astounded by what she saw as an *"underlying order to the universe."* How could this be?[286]

In parallel with her mind-blowing experiences in the lab that summer, she began to think philosophically about God as she read the novel *The Count of Monte Cristo* in her spare time. She was taken by the author's ideas about *"forgiveness and God's role in giving justice."* She was surprised the *"concept of God and religion was not as philosophically trivial"* as she had thought.[287]

That summer during her sophomore year, the **order of the universe** and the philosophical richness of the **concept of God's justice** converged. She wasn't really looking to believe in God, but that was the unintended result.

I stopped in my tracks when it hit me—I believed in God![288]

PETER HITCHENS

Peter Hitchens is the brother of Christopher Hitchens. Like his brother, Peter was raised in a religiously ambivalent non-observant home, educated in British boarding schools,

---

[286]Sarah Salviander, *My Testimony*, SixDay Science, May 11, 2019, https://sixday-science.com/2015/05/11/my-testimony/.
[287]Ibid.
[288]Ibid.

embraced atheism at a young age, and was an advocate of
Marxist communism. He later became a journalist and
traveled the world. As he puts it, he was part of the British
"generation who were too clever to believe" in God:[289]

> *I had replaced Christianity, and the Churchill
> cult, with an elaborate socialist worldview—
> because I had decided that I did not wish to
> believe in God or in patriotism.*[290]

In his mid-thirties, after almost twenty years of being
"physically disgusted"[291] by people who did believe in God,
Peter Hitchens changed his mind. What happened?

- *Loss of faith in a world without God*—Hitchens lost
  faith in a *"Godless universe"* and in *"humanity's ability to achieve justice."*[292] He no longer saw politics and
  his own ambition as something to base his life upon.
- *Accountability*—Hitchens describes that viewing the
  painting *The Last Judgment*, by Rogier van der Wey-
  den, in France caused him to re-encounter and wres-
  tle with the notion of accountability to God.
- *Christmas*—Yes, Christmas. You'll need to read his
  book for the details on this.

Peter Hitchens' rejection of atheism was cemented as a
result of living in an atheist nation. While stationed in
the Soviet Union as a reporter for two years in the early
1990s, he observed Soviet society. The Marxist atheist
utopia he perhaps dreamed of in his youth didn't exist.

---

[289]Peter Hitchens, *The Rage Against God* (Grand Rapids, MI: Zondervan, 2010), 17.
[290]Ibid., 100.
[291]Ibid.
[292]Ibid., 100, 105.

What he saw was a corrupt, harsh *"de-Christianized"* nation where people lived in desperation.[293]

A theistic worldview of an ordered universe with **purpose**, absolute **truth** and absolute **morality** seemed to make sense to Hitchens.

> *I believe in God and the Christian religion at least partly because it suits me to do so. I prefer to believe that I live in an ordered universe with a purpose that I can at least partly discover. I derive my ideas of what is absolutely true and what is absolutely right from this source.*[294]

BARAK LURIE

Barak Lurie grew up as a smart Jewish kid attending good schools in Connecticut. In his family, intellect was emphasized and religion was not. Though Barak's father was Jewish, his father thought organized religion was harmful to society, so he only attended synagogue once per year. The religious void in his family left Barak to reach his own conclusions about God. He did. By the age of eleven he concluded there was none.

> *It's not as if I read Nietzsche at age 11. It wasn't any one influence that brought me to atheism. It was the lack of influences. . . . It was unique about me that I was very interested in God one way or the other. I just chose to not believe in Him.*[295]

---

[293]Ibid., 81–91.

[294]Ibid., 151.

[295]Michael Ashcraft, "Jewish atheist found God at Stanford," God Reports, April 22, 2018, https://blog.godreports.com/2018/04/jewish-atheist-found-god-at-stanford/.

After reaching this conclusion, Barak took a stand and became a vocal advocate for atheism during his middle school and high school years.

As an undergraduate student at Stanford University, Barak selected the *massacres caused by religion* as the topic for his honors thesis. Yet, while doing his research, he realized that the **deaths caused by atheism** during the period he was studying were far larger than those caused by religion. Perhaps belief in God wasn't as bad as he thought—he investigated further.

In his philosophy classes, Barak pondered the idea of **free will** versus determinism. He concluded, if we do have a free will, there actually could be a Creator. He saw the idea of determinism, which is proposed by many atheists and says our actions are only determined by our influences and environment, to be lacking. He states:

> *Once I accepted that I had a free will, I opened the door to the possibility that there was a Creator.*[296]

Barak then started thinking about the possible source of other things—**beauty, love, value, freedom, the desire to do scientific investigation** and **humor**. He also turned his thoughts to the **improbability** that life and a universe like ours exists and found Stephen Hawking's multiverse idea to be lacking in plausibility. As he prepared his thesis, he found that a quote from Fyodor Dostoevsky, a Russian novelist who had rejected his own atheism, struck a chord with him:

---

[296] Ibid.

You cannot truly appreciate God unless you have rejected God.[297]

Through completing his thesis and his studies at Stanford, Barak concluded there is a God. He has since embraced Judaism and actively practices it as his faith.

Barak Lurie is now a successful attorney in Los Angeles. In 2017, he decided to publish a book based on the results of the research for his Stanford thesis. However, the conclusion of the book didn't match the original assumption he held as a college sophomore. So instead, he titled it *Atheism Kills* and it was a best seller on Amazon.

WILLIAM MURRAY

William Murray was raised in a whirlwind of controversy, publicity, litigation and anger unlike anything most of us could even imagine. It was his mother, **Madalyn Murray O'Hair,** who filed the lawsuit that ultimately reached the United States Supreme Court and resulted in state-mandated prayer and Bible reading in public schools to be declared illegal. This happened in 1963 and William, a middle-school student, was the plaintiff in the case. To say he and his mother were disliked by the majority of Americans would be an extreme understatement.

William describes his mother as a disappointed and angry Marxist utopian. After attempting to immigrate to the Soviet Union in 1960 and being rejected, she dedicated herself to American socialist and atheist causes and was the founder of American Atheists.

---

[297] Ibid.

Having been raised in an atheist and socialist home, William willingly embraced both as his default belief-system and was active in his mother's causes.

What causes a man, who spent most of his life in the center of the atheist world, to change his mind and accept theism? In his biography, William describes the **existence of evil** and the **need for a good God** as two key factors.

Through his family life and career, he recognized a level of evil that he could only attribute to a devil:

> *One day, while driving home from work, the truth struck me. I thought, there has to be a god because there certainly is a devil. I have met him, talked to him, and touched him. He is the personification of evil. I've seen him in the lives of people I've known.*[298]

Another key factor was his struggle to overcome severe alcohol addiction. It was at a twelve-step program in Texas, that he was introduced to the idea that God could help him gain sobriety. Since he had already come to the conclusion there was a devil, he found it reasonable to conclude there was *"a good God who could solve troubles and problems."*[299] He accepted the existence of God, started to pray and began to gain victory over alcohol.

The last factor was an unusual experience—a dream. William describes experiencing a dream, sort of along the lines of Emperor Constantine's dramatic vision at the Milvian Bridge in AD 312. While having a nightmare, he saw an angel with a sword cut his dream in half and then, with

---

[298]William Murray, *My Life Without God* (Washington, DC: WND Books, 2012), 265.
[299]Ibid., 270.

the sword, touch an open Bible. On the handle of the sword was the Latin phrase, IN HOC SIGNO VINCE ("By this symbol conquer.")

To William, the dream wasn't random. He saw it as a personal revelation from God pointing him to read the Bible. It was after buying a Bible at a late-night department store and reading the Gospel of Luke that he then accepted Christianity. This happened in 1980, when he was thirty-three years old.[300]

The son of the most famous and disliked atheist in America changed his mind and came to believe in God. Go figure.

SARAH IRVING-STONEBRAKER

Sarah Irving-Stonebraker isn't a celebrity or a rock star. She's not a nineteenth-century philosopher, a dead poet or a Nobel Prize winner. She hasn't even been at the center of an international controversy. She's merely an accomplished university history professor in Australia. What's interesting about her is the intellectual journey she took as a former atheist who changed her mind.

Like many atheists, Sarah's family in Australia was non-religious. She describes herself as having generally been critical of all religion. She was also academically talented. After completing her undergraduate studies at the University of Sydney, she won a scholarship to perform PhD studies in history at Kings College in Cambridge University in England. While there, she found her views of religion, and specifically of Christianity, to fit in quite well:

---

[300]Ibid., 279–80.

> *King's is known for its secular ideology and my perception of Christianity fitted well with the views of my fellow students: Christians were anti-intellectual and self-righteous.*[301]

Sarah didn't begin to question her atheism until a few years later. She had completed her PhD in 2007 and was a Junior Research Fellow at Oxford University. It was there that she attended three guest lectures by atheist philosopher Peter Singer.

Singer discussed the challenge of ascribing equal worth to human life where human capabilities differ. For example, is the value of a disabled child's life the same as that of a healthy child? From the perspective of naturalism, the answer is "no." The lectures left her disturbed. To her, the notion that human worth was subjective undermined the very foundation of morality.

> *I began to realise that the implications of my atheism were incompatible with almost every value I held dear.*[302]

Not long after Singer's lectures, while doing research in the university library, she found herself near the theology section. Out of curiosity, she selected a book and began to read the sermons of Paul Tillich, a famous theologian. She was struck by his substantial intellect and left interested and open to the idea of God's existence. However, she was not yet convinced.

---

[301]Sarah Irving-Stonebraker, "How Oxford and Peter Singer drove me from atheism to Jesus," (Cambridge, MA: Veritas Forum, 2018), http://www.veritas.org/oxford-atheism-to-jesus/.

[302]http://www.veritas.org/oxford-atheism-to-jesus/

She was further prodded by a professor of nanomaterials, who was a Christian, whom she met at a dinner. He challenged her to not "*sit on the fence*" about God. She realized that, if her beliefs about human worth were really important to her, she needed to resolve in her mind whether God exists.[303]

In 2008, Sarah accepted a position as an assistant history professor at Florida State University. She observed that the Christians she came to know in Florida seemed to actually value people and live morally. They volunteered at community centers, fed the homeless, and helped migrant laborers. It was there that, as a twenty-seven-year-old, she started attending church. Through the sermons and her own study, she came to accept the existence of God and that God unconditionally loved her.

The final clincher for Sarah was reading C. S. Lewis' *Mere Christianity*. After reading it, alone in her apartment, she embraced the idea of God and became a Christian.

IAN HUTCHINSON

Ian Hutchinson is an expert in plasma physics and a professor of nuclear science at the Massachusetts Institute of Technology. He headed MIT's nuclear fusion research, authored 200 scientific research articles and headed peer review for a scientific journal. Based on a brief phone conversation I had with him a few years ago, he seems to be a very gracious, soft-spoken, research scientist.

As a child, Ian Hutchinson didn't believe in God and wasn't raised in a religious home. Though he was educated in a British boarding school with a religious tradition, it had no impact on his beliefs. He just assumed there was no

---

[303]Ibid.

God and the subject didn't seem to be of particular importance to him.

His exploration of the idea of God occurred in a calm logical manner while he was an undergraduate physics student at Cambridge University.

At Cambridge, Ian initially wasn't particularly interested in religion in general or the specific faith of Christianity.

> . . . *the self-congratulatory attitude among the enlightened (including me) was that Christianity had been discovered to be irrelevant and outdated.*[304]

However, Ian valued **morality** and it disturbed him that modern society and academic institutions, in spite of advancements in science and technology, were "*if anything, doing a worse job at developing and sustaining the virtues that I valued: truth, integrity, rationality, compassion.*"[305]

Ian's serious consideration of God and Christianity began through interactions with two close friends at Cambridge who were serious Christians. While Ian "*had some appreciation of Jesus as a moral teacher and a compelling historical figure,*" he hadn't really considered whether the story about Jesus was true.[306]

This caused him to investigate and ponder the **historical evidence** for the life of Jesus. His reasoned conclusion was that there was sufficient evidence to accept Christianity as true. So, without any drama or crisis, he became a Christian.

While finishing his studies at Cambridge and then doing PhD studies in Australia, Ian continued to ponder evidence

---

[304]Ian Hutchinson, *Can a Scientist Believe in Miracles?* (Downers Grove, IL: InterVarsity Press, 2018), 5.
[305]Ibid.
[306]Ibid., 6.

and to challenge his own faith. He also assessed his belief in God versus his role as a scientist. He saw no conflict between his belief in God and his scientific pursuits then and still sees no conflict now.

JOY DAVIDMAN

Joy Davidman was a child prodigy. She scored off the charts on IQ tests, could play a Chopin piano score after reading it once, entered college at the age of fifteen, and earned a masters degree from Columbia University when she was twenty. That was in 1935. She then became a poet, novelist and film critic. And, though born into a New York Jewish family, she and her father were ardent atheists.

Davidman, disillusioned with capitalism during the Great Depression, became a Communist and married a fellow Communist. Their marriage was a disaster from the start. Her husband, who turned out to be a serial adulterer and alcoholic, was absent for extended periods of time while she stayed at home caring for their two sons. At one point, he even had an affair with her cousin who was staying with them. Communism, which she left, was a disappointment. Her marriage was worse.

What caused Joy Davidman to change her mind about atheism was what she described as the **presence of God**. It was during a period of crisis, while she was angry, alone with her infant sons, and in despair, that she lowered her guard against God. She described what she then experienced as a brief unexpected encounter with God's presence:

> *It is infinite, unique; there are no words, there are no comparisons. Can one scoop up the sea in a teacup? Those who have known God will understand me.... There was a Person with me in that*

> *room, directly present to my consciousness—a*
> *Person so real that all my previous life was by*
> *comparison a mere shadow play. And I myself*
> *was more alive than I had ever been; it was like*
> *waking from sleep.*[307]

After having this experience, she concluded there is a God and began to investigate. Her search started with Reform Judaism and culminated in her becoming a Christian. It was while reading the Gospels that she again experienced God's presence. She concluded that "*he was Jesus.*"[308]

Her marriage to her unfaithful husband ultimately ended in divorce. She would later marry another famous former atheist, C. S. Lewis.

[307]Lyle W. Dorsett, *And God Came In* (Peabody, MA: Hendrickson, 2011), 60.
[308]Lyle W. Dorsett, "Helen Joy Davidman (Mrs. C. S. Lewis) 1915–1960: A Portrait" (Springfield, VA: C. S. Lewis Institute, 2018), http://www.cslewisinstitute.org/node/31.

A FEW PARTING
THOUGHTS

Bold assertions proclaimed repeatedly, loudly or even angrily may fill a room with noise but that doesn't make them true. Truth is something that can be sought with humility and grace; it doesn't require anger or insults. It can stand on its own and isn't something to be feared, unless we're unwilling to be changed by it.

Many of the things that atheists confidently affirm make no sense. Unfortunately, not everything they say is based on perfect information and reason nor is it without bias. Like everyone else, they're only human. There actually are scientific, historical, moral, philosophical, and experiential reasons to conclude that God does exist. This reasoned conclusion need not be based on blind faith. We all have minds and are free to use them.

What makes sense?—A key question for us all to ask is, "What makes the most sense?" Does a universe like ours, which had a beginning and which operates based upon finely tuned laws, make more sense with or without an ultimate cause—a creator? Does the existence of life—all of which looks as though it was designed—that depends upon large amounts of purposeful information, programs and integrated processes, make more sense with or without a designer?

Do our concepts of human worth, morals and purpose make more sense with or without a universal standard? Does human consciousness that extends beyond death make more sense with or without an ultimate conscious source? In summary, does the universe we know and live in make more sense with or without God? My reasoned conclusion is that a universe with God makes more sense.

Our pursuit of truth—Perhaps it's appropriate for one of the final thoughts in this discourse to be from one who may have pondered the subject of God a bit longer than I. I leave you with a wise observation by Peter Hitchens:

> *Once you have convinced a fellow-creature of the rightness of a cause, he takes his own direction and lives his own life. It is quite likely that even if you change your mind, he will not change his. Yet you remain at least partly responsible for what he does. Those who write where many listen, had best be careful what they say. Someone is bound to take them seriously, and it really is no good pretending that you didn't know this.*[309]

No matter what position we believe to be true, we are well served to do so with humility, kindness and good intent. And, as Peter Hitchens says, we bear some responsibility for what others do with the positions we espouse and even the manner in which we espouse them.

If God exists, and I thoroughly believe this to be the case, seeking to know God and his plan for humanity is likely the most noble endeavor we can pursue. However, as we pursue this noble endeavor, let us do so nobly.

---

[309]Peter Hitchens, *The Rage Against God* (Grand Rapids, MI: Zondervan, 2010), 21.

APPENDIX ONE: SUGGESTIONS FOR FURTHER READING

There are many great sources that deal with the topics covered in this book. Here are just a few I found to be both helpful and enjoyable.

SCIENCE

Michael Behe, *The Edge of Evolution*
Stephen Meyer, *Darwin's Doubt*
John Lennox, *God's Undertaker*
Fazale Rana, *The Cell's Design*
Ian Hutchinson, *Can a Scientist Believe in Miracles?*

PHILOSOPHY AND MODERN CULTURE

Antony Flew, *There Is a God*
Peter Hitchens, *The Rage Against God*

HISTORICAL CHRISTIANITY

C. S. Lewis, *Mere Christianity*

APPENDIX TWO: SOURCES CITED

Appian, *The Roman History of Appian of Alexandria: The Foreign Wars*, trans. Horace White (London: George Bell and Sons, 1899)

Michael Ashcraft, "Jewish atheist found God at Stanford," God Reports, April 22, 2018, https://blog.godreports.com/2018/04/jewish-atheist-found-god-at-stanford/

Babylonian Talmud, Tractate Sanhedrin (43a), (London: Soncino Press, 1987)

Nigel Barber, "Is Religion Better at Making Peace or Making War?, *Psychology Today*, August 1, 2012, https://www.psychologytoday.com/us/blog/the-human-beast/201208/is-religion-better-making-peace-or-making-war

Michael Behe, *The Edge of Evolution* (New York: Free Press, 2008)

Susan Blakemore, *Consciousness: A Very Short Introduction* (Oxford, England: Oxford University Press, 2017)

F. F. Bruce, *The New Testament Documents: Are They Reliable?* (Downers Grove, IL: Intervarsity Press, 1960)

Ludwig Büchner, *Force and Matter* (New York: Peter Eckler, 1891)

David Chalmers, *The Conscious Mind: In Search of a Fundamental Theory* (New York: Oxford University Press, 1996)

Cicero, *The Republic and The Laws* (Oxford, England: Oxford University Press, 2008)

Francis Collins, *The Language of God* (New York: Free Press, 2007)

Francis Crick, *Life Itself: Its Origin and Nature* (New York: Simon & Schuster, 1981)

Paul Davies, *The Goldilocks Enigma* (Boston, MA: Houghton Mifflin Co., 2006)

Paul Davies, *The Mind of God* (New York: Simon and Schuster, 1992)

Richard Dawkins, *Atheists for Jesus*, https://www.rationalresponders.com/atheists_for_jesus_ a_richard_dawkins_essay

Richard Dawkins, *The Blind Watchmaker* (New York: W. W. Norton & Company, 1986)

Richard Dawkins, *The God Delusion* (New York: Mariner Books, 2008)

Neil deGrasse Tyson: "Doctors," The Amazing Meeting, Keynote Speech, 2008, https://www.youtube.com/playlist?list=PLBDBC78EF8B22B179

Frank Dikötter, *Mao's Great Leap to Famine*, New York Times, December 15, 2010, http://www.nytimes.com/2010/12/16/opinion/16iht-eddikotter16.html

Lyle W. Dorsett, *And God Came In* (Peabody, MA: Hendrickson, 2011)

Lyle W. Dorsett, "Helen Joy Davidman (Mrs. C. S. Lewis) 1915–1960: A Portrait" (Springfield, VA: C. S. Lewis Institute, 2018), http://www.cslewisinstitute.org/node/31

Freeman Dyson, *Disturbing the Universe* (New York: Basic Books, 1979)

John C. Eccles, *Evolution of the Brain: Creation of the Soul*, (New York: Routledge, 1989)

Epicurus, *The Extant Remains* (Oxford, England: Clarendon Press, 1926)

Eutropius, *Abridgement of Roman History* (London: George Bell and Sons, 1886)

Antony Flew, *There Is a God* (New York: HarperCollins, 2007)

Vensus George, *Authentic Human Destiny, The Paths of Shankara and Heidegger* (Washington, DC: The Council for Research in Values and Philosophy, 1998)

Neil Gross and Solon Simmons, "The Religiosity of American College and University Professors," *Sociology of Religion*, 2009, 70:2

Ernst Haeckel, *The Wonders of Life* (London: Watts & Co., 1904)

Sam Harris, *Letter to a Christian Nation* (New York: Alfred A. Knopf, 2006)

Sam Harris, *The End of Faith* (New York: W.W. Horton & Co., 2005)

Stephen Hawking, *Brief Answers to the Big Questions* (New York: Bantam Books, 2018)

Stephen Hawking, *The Grand Design* (New York: Bantam Books, 2012)

Christopher Hitchens, *God Is Not Great* (New York: Hachette Book Group, 2009)

Peter Hitchens, *The Rage Against God* (Grand Rapids, MI: Zondervan, 2010)

John Horgan, "Physicist George Ellis Knocks Physicists for Knocking Philosophy, Falsification, Free Will," *Scientific American* (July 22, 2014) https://blogs.scientificamerican.com/cross-check/physicist-george-ellis-knocks-physicists-for-knocking-philosophy-falsification-free-will/

Fred Hoyle and Chandra Wickramasinghe, *Evolution from Space* (New York: Touchstone, 1981)

Fred Hoyle, *The Intelligent Universe* (New York: Holt, Reinhart and Winston, 1983)

David Hume, *Dialogues Concerning Natural Religion*, (London: 1779)

Ian Hutchinson, *Can a Scientist Believe in Miracles?* (Downers Grove, IL: InterVarsity Press, 2018)

Ian Hutchinson, *Monopolizing Knowledge* (Belmont, MA: Fias Publishing, 2011)

Max Jaeger, "Texas church shooter was a militant atheist," *NY Post*, November 6, 2017, https://nypost.com/2017/11/06/ex-friends-say-shooter-was-creepy-atheist-who-berated-religious-people/

Josephus, *The Works of Josephus*, trans. William Whiston (Peabody, MA: Hendrickson, 1987)

Gordon Kane, "Are virtual particles really constantly popping in and out of existence? Or are they merely a mathematical bookkeeping device for quantum mechanics?" *Scientific American*, October 9, 2006, https://www.scientificamerican.com/article/are-virtual-particles-rea/?redirect=1

Edward F. Kelly, Emily Williams Kelly, et al., *Irreducible Mind: Toward a Psychology for the 21st Century* (New York: Rowan & Littlefield Publishers, Inc., 2007)

Søren Kierkegaard, *Fear and Anxiety* (Princeton, NJ: Princeton University Press, 1954)

Søren Kierkegaard, *The Concept of Anxiety* (New York: Liveright Publishing Corp., 2014)

George Klein, *The Atheist and the Holy City* (Cambridge, MA: The MIT Press, 1990)

Sarah Knapton, "First hint of 'life after death' in biggest ever scientific study," *Telegraph* (London, England: Telegraph Media Group Ltd., October 7, 2014), http://www.telegraph.co.uk/science/2016/03/12/first-hint-of-life-after-death-in-biggest-ever-scientific-study/

Paul Kurtz, *Forbidden Fruit: The Ethics of Humanism* (Buffalo, NY: Prometheus Books, 1988)

Paul Kurtz, *Humanist Manifesto 2000* (Amherst, NY: Prometheus Press, 2000)

Kurtis Lee, "Memorial Day: The number of Americans who have died in battle since the Revolutionary War," *The Los Angeles Times*, May 29, 2017, http://www.latimes.com/nation/la-na-memorial-day-20170529-htmlstory.html

Gottfried Wilhelm Leibniz, *The Philosophical Works of Leibnitz* (New Haven, CT: Tuttle, Morehouse & Taylor Publishers, 1890)

John Lennox, *God and Stephen Hawking* (Oxford, England: Lion Hudson, 2011)

C. S. Lewis, *Mere Christianity* (New York: HarperOne, 2001)

Alan Lurie, "Is Religion the Cause of Most Wars?" *Huffington Post*, June 10, 2012, https://www.huffingtonpost.com/rabbi-alan-lurie/is-religion-the-cause-of-_b_1400766.html

Karl Marx, *Critique of Hegel's Philosophy of Right*, ed. Joseph O'Malley (Oxford, England: Oxford University Press, 1970)

Colin McGinn, *Physics and Physicalism*, January 28, 2019, http://www.colinmcginn.net/physics-and-physicalism/#.XNWKYRRKhpg

Colin McGinn, *The Mysterious Flame* (New York: Basic Books, 1999)

Alister McGrath, "Breaking the Science-Atheism Bond," http://www.beliefnet.com/news/science-religion/2005/08/breaking-the-science-atheism-bond.aspx

Alister McGrath, "Science Turned Me Away from Atheism," https://www.youtube.com/watch?v=-s7n9PYTtSM, 1-1-2018

Merriam-Webster Online Dictionary, © 2015 by Merriam-Webster, Inc., https://www.merriam-webster.com/dictionary

Stephen Meyer, *Darwin's Doubt* (New York: HarperOne, 2013)

Stephen Meyer, *Signature in the Cell* (New York: HarperOne, 2009)

Jamgön Mipham, *White Lotus, An Explanation of the Seven-Line Prayer to Guru Padmasambhava* (Boston, MA: Shambhala Publications, 2007)

Jacques Monod, *Chance and Necessity* (New York: Alfred A. Knopf, 1971)

Clara Moskowitz, "Are We Living in a Computer Simulation?" *Scientific American*, April 7, 2016, https://www.scientificamerican.com/article/are-we-living-in-a-computer-simulation/

William Murray, *My Life Without God* (Washington, DC: WND Books, 2012)

Seth Mydans, "Death of Pol Pot," *New York Times*, April 17, 1998, https://www.nytimes.com/1998/04/17/world/death-pol-pot-pol-pot-brutal-dictator-who-forced-cambodians-killing-fields-dies.html

Thomas Nagel, *Mind & Cosmos—Why the Materialist Neo-Darwinian Conception of Nature Is Almost Certainly Wrong* (New York: Oxford University Press, 2012)

Thomas Nagel, *The Last Word* (New York: Oxford University Press, 1997)

Kai Nielson, *Ethics without God* (Amherst, NY: Prometheus Books, 1990)

New World Encyclopedia, http://www.newworldencyclopedia.org

Friedrich Nietzsche, *Beyond Good and Evil* (New York: MacMillan Company, 1907)

Friedrich Nietzsche, *Joyful Wisdom* (New York: Frederick Unger Publishing, 1960)

Friedrich Nietzsche, *The AntiChrist* (New York: Alfred A. Knopf, 1920)

Friedrich Nietzsche, *Twilight of the Idols and The Antichrist*, (Middlesex, England; Penguin Books, 1969)

Mary Anastasia O'Grady, "Counting Castro's Victims," *Wall Street Journal*, December 30, 2005, https://www.wsj.com/articles/SB113590852154334404

Michael Onfray, *Atheist Manifesto* (New York: Arcade Publishing, 2011)

Origen, *Against Celsus*, Alexander Roberts & James Donaldson, Ante-Nicene Fathers, Vol. 4 (Peabody, MA: Hendrickson, 1999),

Roger Penrose, *The Emperor's New Mind* (Oxford, England: Oxford University Press, 2016)

Pew Research Center:

—"In America, Does More Education Equal Less Religion?" Pew Research Center, April 26, 2017, http://www.pewforum. org/2017/04/26/in-america-does-more-education-equal-less-religion/

—"Millennial Generation Less Religiously active than Older Americans" (Washington, DC, Pew Research Center, 2010), https://www.pewforum.org/2010/02/17/millennial-genera-tion-less-religiously-active-than-older-americans/

—"Religious Landscape Study" (Washington, DC: Pew Research Center, 2014), http://www.pewforum.org/religious-land-scape-study/

—"When Americans Say They Believe in God, What Do They Mean?" Pew Research Center, April 25, 2018, http://www. pewforum.org/2018/04/25/when-americans-say-they-believe-in-god-what-do-they-mean/

Shlomo Pines, *An Arabic Version of the Testimonium Flavium and Its Implications* (Jerusalem, Jerusalem Academic Press, 1971)

Max Planck, *The Philosophy of Physics* (New York: W. W. Norton, 1936)

Max Planck, *Where Is Science Going?* (New York: W. W. Norton, 1932)

Pliny The Younger, *Complete Letters* (New York: Oxford University Press, 2006)

William M. Ramsay, *The Bearing of Recent Discovery on the Trustworthiness of the New Testament* (Grand Rapids, MI: Baker Book House, 1953)

Fazale Rana, *The Cell's Design* (Grand Rapids, MI: Baker Books, 2008)

Ayn Rand, *The Virtue of Selfishness* (New York: Signet Books, 1964)

Alex Rosenberg, *The Atheist's Guide to Reality* (New York: W. W. Norton & Company, 2011)

Bertrand Russell, *Religion and Science* (New York: Oxford University Press, 1997)

Bertrand Russell, *Why I Am Not a Christian* (New York: Simon & Schuster, 1957)

Sarah Salviander, "God, the expanding universe, and dark energy," https://sixdayscience.com/, January 23, 2019

Sarah Salviander, "My Testimony," SixDay Science, May 11, 2019, https://sixdayscience.com/2015/05/11/my-testimony/, January 23, 2019

Gerald Schroeder, *The Hidden Face of God* (New York: Touchstone, 2001)

Rupert Sheldrake, *The Science Delusion: Freeing the Spirit of Enquiry* (London: Hodder & Stoughton, 2012)

Michael Shermer with Colin McGinn - "Mysterianism, Consciousness, Free Will & God," July 16, 2018, https://www.youtube.com/watch?v=twrQk-eF2r4

Ethan Siegel, "Dark Energy May Not Be a Constant, Which Would Lead to a Revolution in Physics," *Forbes*, January 31, 2019, https://www.forbes.com/sites/startswithabang/2019/01/31/dark-energy-may-not-be-a-constant-which-would-lead-to-a-revolution-in-physics/#52266b3ab737

Peter Singer, *How Are We to Live?: Ethics in an Age of Self-Interest* (Amherst, NY: Prometheus Books, 1995)

Peter Singer, *Rethinking Life and Death* (New York: St. Martin's Griffin, 1994)

Peter Singer, *The Expanding Circle: Ethics, Evolution and Moral Progress* (Princeton, NJ: Princeton University Press, 2011)

Timothy Snyder, "Hitler vs. Stalin: Who Killed More?", *New York Review of Books*, 3-10-2011, http://www.nybooks.com/articles/2011/03/10/hitler-vs-stalin-who-killed-more/

Victor Stenger, *God: The Failed Hypothesis* (Amherst, NY: Prometheus Books, 2007)

Sarah Irving-Stonebraker, "How Oxford and Peter Singer drove me from atheism to Jesus" (Cambridge, MA: Veritas Forum, 2018), http://www.veritas.org/oxford-atheism-to-jesus/

Suetonius, *Lives of the Twelve Caesars* (London: Wordsworth Editions Ltd, 1997)

Tacitus, *Annals* (Oxford, England: Oxford University Press, 2008)

Tacitus, *The Histories* (London: Penguin Classics, 2009)

Yeshe Tsogyal, Erik Pema Kunsang (Translator), *The Lotus-Born: The Life Story of Padamasambhava* (Hong Kong, Rangjung Yeshe Publications, 1998)

United States government –

—*America's Wars* (Washington, DC: U.S. Dept. of Veterans Affairs, 2017), https://www.va.gov/opa/publications/factsheets/fs_americas_wars.pdf

—*Revelations from the Russian Archives, Anti-Religious Campaigns* (Washington, DC: U.S. Library of Congress, 2010), https://www.loc.gov/exhibits/archives/anti.html

—*2013 Hate Crime Statistics* (Washington, DC: U.S. Department of Justice, 2013), https://ucr.fbi.gov/hate-crime/2013/topic-pages/victims/victims_final

J. Warner Wallace, *Cold-Case Christianity: A Homicide Detective Investigates the Claims of the Gospels* (Colorado Springs: David C. Cook, 2013)

Richard Weikart, *From Darwin to Hitler* (New York: Palgrave MacMillan, 2004)

Steven Weinberg, *The First Three Minutes* (New York: Basic Books, 1993)

Ngawang Zangpo, *Guru Rinpoché—His Life and Times*, (Ithaca, NY: Snow Lion Publications, 2002)

Additional websites referenced:

—http://www.bbc.co.uk/blogs/ni/2009/03/michael_reiss_why_i_resigned_f.html
—https://www.theguardian.com/commentisfree/andrewbrown/2011/jul/04/harry-kroto-science-truth
—http://www.muktinath.org/buddhism/padmasambhava.pdf
—http://www.mylifetime.com/movies/i-survived-beyond-and-back